IMAGES
of America

AROUND GUNNISON
AND CRESTED BUTTE

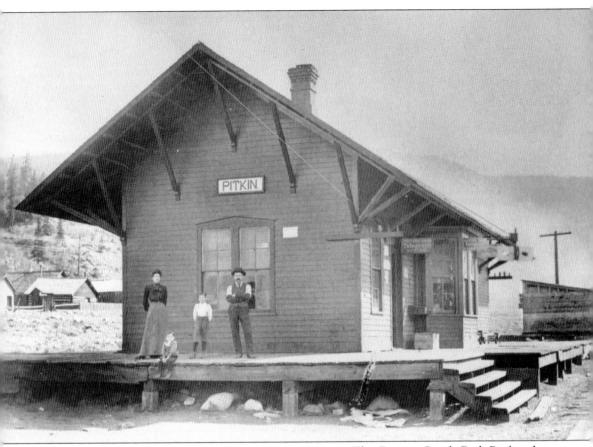

Denver South Park and Pacific Depot, Pitkin. The Denver South Park Railroad ran from Denver through South Park and through the Continental Divide via the Alpine Tunnel. From there, the narrow gauge slowly dropped over 2,000 feet in 13 miles before arriving in the much-heralded silver camp of Pitkin. With a railroad, smelters, high-paying mines, and investors flocking in, Pitkin was headed for greatness. Lack of high-grade ore and the silver panic of 1893 marked the end of Pitkin's dreams.

On the Cover: A lone skier navigates the powder snow on Monument, an extreme run at the Mount Crested Butte Ski Area, in the early 1970s. The steep and rugged terrain of the Elk Mountains is visible in the background. The discovery of silver in this region in the 1880s brought in thousands of miners, narrow-gauge railroads, and smelters. Crested Butte became the center of activity—"the Gateway to the Elk Mountains." (Courtesy Mount Crested Butte Ski Area.)

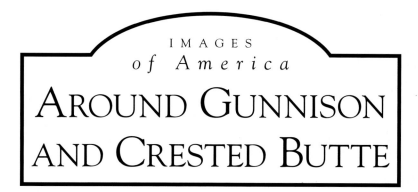

IMAGES of America
AROUND GUNNISON AND CRESTED BUTTE

Duane Vandenbusche, the Gunnison Pioneer Museum,
and the Crested Butte Mountain Heritage Museum

ARCADIA
PUBLISHING

Copyright © 2008 by Duane Vandenbusche, the Gunnison Pioneer Museum, and the Crested Butte Mountain Heritage Museum
ISBN 978-0-7385-4828-9

Published by Arcadia Publishing
Charleston SC, Chicago IL, Portsmouth NH, San Francisco CA

Printed in the United States of America

Library of Congress Catalog Card Number: 2007933016

For all general information contact Arcadia Publishing at:
Telephone 843-853-2070
Fax 843-853-0044
E-mail sales@arcadiapublishing.com
For customer service and orders:
Toll-Free 1-888-313-2665

Visit us on the Internet at www.arcadiapublishing.com

This book is dedicated to Western State College distance runners, all of whom have inspired me.

Contents

Acknowledgments		6
Introduction		7
1.	The Hub of the Wheel	9
2.	Jewel of the Elk Mountains	21
3.	Silver, Hot Springs, and Gold	39
4.	The Great North Country	51
5.	Little Engines That Could	65
6.	Ski Country	75
7.	Of Mines and Men	85
8.	Cattle Kings and Mining Men	95
9.	The Black Canyon	105
10.	Potpourri	117
Bibliography		127

Acknowledgments

Many thanks go to the Gunnison Pioneer Museum and the Crested Butte Mountain Heritage Museum for the use of the photographs in this book. Unless otherwise noted, all images come from these collections and also from the Gunnison Country old-timers. Special appreciation goes to C. J. Miller, president of the board of the Gunnison Pioneer Museum, and Glo Cunningham and Melissa Belz, executive director and curator of the Crested Butte Mountain Heritage Museum, respectively. All three were generous with their time, historical knowledge, and suggestions.

The Gunnison and Crested Butte communities, along with the members and volunteers of the two museums, are to be praised for supporting the museums since their beginnings in 1964 and 2003. Both have preserved the rich heritage of Gunnison, Crested Butte, and the Gunnison Country. The Gunnison Pioneer Museum has as its centerpieces the historic Paragon School and the Denver and Rio Grande narrow-gauge engine No. 268. The Crested Butte Mountain Heritage Museum is housed in the historic Tony's Conoco Gas Station on Elk Avenue. Both facilities are rich in artifacts, scrapbooks, photographs, and primary source material.

Through the years, my interviews of old-timers like Craig Goodwin, Bruce Hartman, Dave Howard, Rial Lake, Lyle McNeill, Whitey Sporcich, Fred Winters, Grant Youmans, and many others have greatly added to the information in this book. The memoirs of Alonzo Hartman and Harry Cornwell, dating back to the 1870s and 1880s, and the early research and writings of Betty Wallace were also extremely valuable to me.

I am very grateful for the support, guidance, and patience of editor Hannah Carney and Arcadia Publishing.

Lastly, I thank my father, a Belgian immigrant, and my mother, who grew up in rural Wisconsin—neither having had a high school education—for instilling in me the love and importance of learning. And for all the old-timers of the Gunnison Country: a special salute for the kindness and information you have so generously given me.

INTRODUCTION

The Gunnison Country, dominated by the towns of Gunnison and Crested Butte, is a stunningly beautiful mountain paradise on Colorado's Western Slope. The region is characterized by high alpine valleys surrounded by the 14,000-foot-high mountains of the San Juan, Elk, and Sawatch Ranges. Archaeological digs have proved the existence of native peoples 12,000 years ago. Ute Indians had their summer home in the Gunnison Country more than 350 years ago. Legal and illegal Spanish expeditions passed through the region as early as the 1600s looking for traces of gold. Names carved on trees, rusting mining tools, and early Spanish names of mountains, rivers, and passes bear witness to the influence of Spain.

When Spain's forays into the Gunnison Country ended, the fur trader or mountain man followed seeking "black gold." Ezekiel Williams and Antoine Robidoux are only two of the many trappers who crossed the Continental Divide into the challenging environment of the mysterious land to the west. Heavy snows, temperatures that dipped to 50 degrees below zero, hostile Ute Indians, and long distances from supply lines ended the fur-trading frontier by 1840.

The need for a railroad to tie the Midwest with the new state of California led to Capt. John Gunnison's ill-fated 1853 expedition to the West. Gunnison surveyed a central railroad route between the 38th and 39th parallels and made his way through the country that would soon have his name. He was killed by Paiute Indians in southwest Utah in October 1853.

By 1860, only a little was known about the Gunnison Country, but persistent rumors of gold were prevalent. This led to the placer mining decade from 1860 to 1870. Despite the Ute Indians, a short mining season because of extreme weather conditions, and isolation, up to a thousand placer miners came to the Gunnison Country during that 10-year span. They panned every stream and took out over $1 million of gold. Some spoke in hushed terms of Taylor Park, Washington Gulch, Lottis Creek, Snowblind Gulch, Deadman's Gulch, and other great locations.

The placer mining era ended around 1870 and after a short lull came the promise of silver. In the late 1870s, miners came into the Gunnison Country via a series of high passes from Leadville and other silver camps on the east side of the Continental Divide. By 1882, some 25,000 to 40,000 miners had streamed in in search of silver and gold. Major silver camps sprang up. The most promising were Gothic, Irwin, White Pine, Tin Cup, and Pitkin. At their peak, all had transient populations of 2,000 to 4,000 people. However, the two most important camps were Gunnison and Crested Butte, both of which became supply, railroad, and smelter towns.

When the silver panic of 1893 destroyed the majority of the silver camps, Crested Butte and Gunnison survived. Crested Butte then turned to coal mining and Gunnison to ranching. Crested Butte was one of the great coal towns in Colorado from the 1880s to 1952 when the coal mines shut down. A decade later, the old coal town embarked on a new era: the age of snow. Two transplanted Kansans—Dick Eflin and Fred Rice—started the Crested Butte Ski Area, and it became the lifeblood of the town. From near ghost-town status in 1952, Crested Butte rose from the ashes and began to thrive. Today the town and Mount Crested Butte, located at the ski area, are thriving with thousands of skiers every year, a great tourist industry, and progressive land development.

Gunnison has not experienced the growth of Crested Butte but instead has the Blue Mesa Reservoir, Colorado's second largest tourist attraction, lying nine miles west of town and Western State College with its 2,500 students. Only 14,000 people live in the Gunnison Country, and it ranks as one of the most affluent counties in the United States. Today the Gunnison Country is one of the best kept secrets in Colorado and the American West, providing world-class skiing, mountain biking, hunting, fishing, and mountain climbing at one's door.

Gunnison, Crested Butte, and the Gunnison Country remain off the beaten path, little changed compared to the other mountain areas of the West and Colorado. The two mountain towns were in the past and remain today jewels of the Rocky Mountains.

One

THE HUB OF THE WHEEL

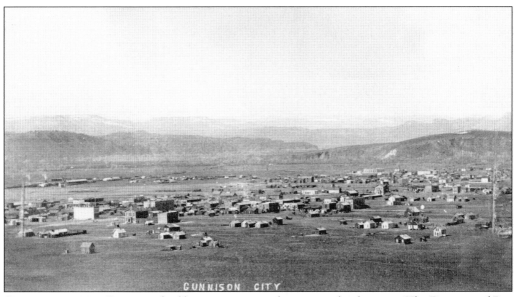

GUNNISON, 1881. Gunnison had become a roaring boomtown by this time. The Denver and Rio Grande Railroad arrived in August, the population reached 3,500, and a building boom was in full force. Thousands from all walks of life came to Gunnison, with many living in tents. Saloons, gambling dens, and houses of prostitution did a thriving business night after night. Residents hoped that the new town would become a city, and some even believed Gunnison was destined to become the capital of Colorado.

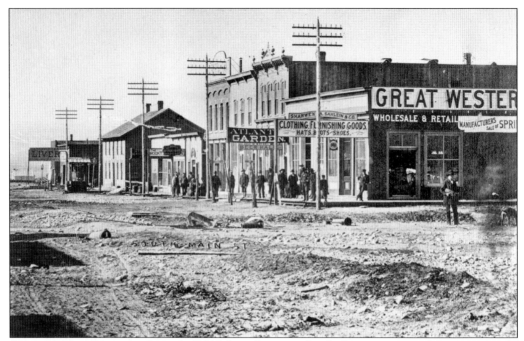

SOUTH MAIN STREET, 1882. At 7,703 feet above sea level, Gunnison soon became a supply town for the many nearby mining camps surrounding it. The town was known as "the Hub of the Wheel" because roads ran from it to the promising camps of Gothic, White Pine, Pitkin, Tin Cup, and Irwin.

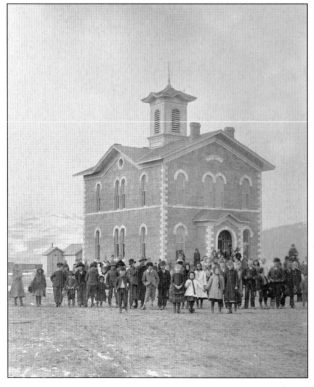

GUNNISON'S FIRST PUBLIC SCHOOL. This school, ostentatious for its time, was built of brick in 1881 for $5,500. By the end of its first year, it was accommodating over 100 students.

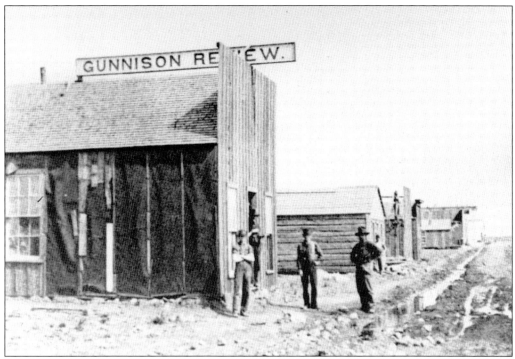

GUNNISON REVIEW OFFICE, 1880. This newspaper was one of the first in town, becoming a daily during the boom days. When the boom faded, the *Gunnison Review* was renamed the *Gunnison Tribune* and made a weekly again.

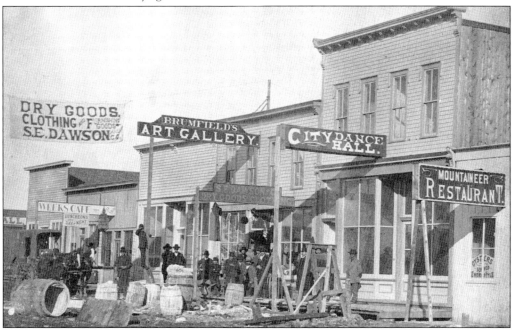

S. E. DAWSON'S DRY GOODS STORE. It was not uncommon for goods to be dumped together in the middle of the street in the halcyon boom days. Merchants were then forced to search for their consignment.

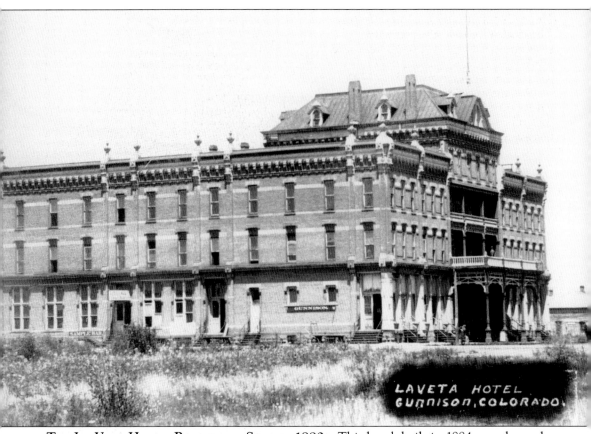

THE LA VETA HOTEL, BOULEVARD STREET, 1880S. This hotel, built in 1884, was deemed a "peacock among mud hens" by travellers. It cost $250,000 and was four and a half stories high with 107 rooms. The La Veta had crystal chandeliers, Persian rugs, and teak and mahogany furniture. The hotel's fortunes slowly waned until it was sold at a 1943 sheriff's sale for $8,350. Nothing remains today.

HUGE CLOCK IN THE LA VETA HOTEL. The clock advertised the perpetual sunshine in Gunnison. The La Veta gave a free meal or room to any guest on any day the sun did not appear. From 1910 to 1927, the sun did not shine at all on a mere nine days. Owner J. H. Howland took a lot of money from his guests, betting on the sun.

MAIN STREET, 1882. The streets in town were very wide to handle the tremendous number of freighters and stage lines that came to the Gunnison Country in an endless stream throughout the 1880s.

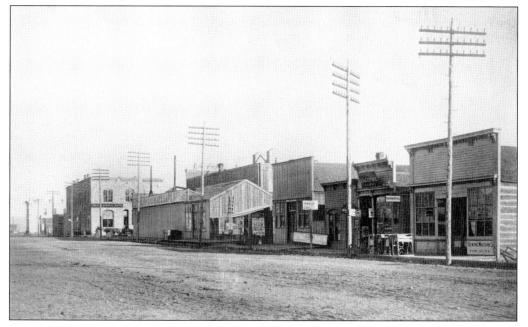

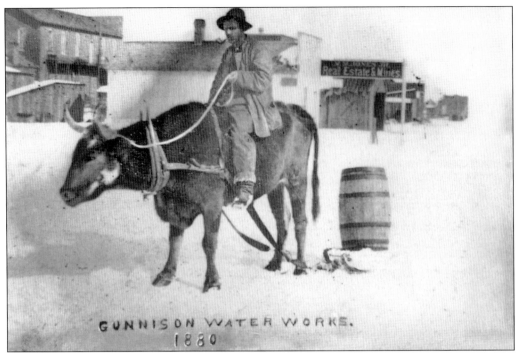

"DOBE JOHN," GUNNISON'S FIRST WATERWORKS, 1880. This colorful character rode a flop-eared cow, which pulled a barrel of water mounted on a sled, to individual customers around town. He got his water from a large well in the middle of Main Street and peddled it for $1 a barrel.

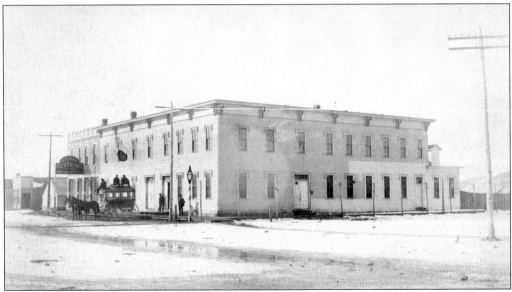

THE MULLIN HOUSE, GUNNISON'S ONLY FIRST-CLASS HOTEL. This hotel spanned 75 by 94 feet, rose two stories high, and cost $24,000 to build in 1880. It included 40 rooms, a barbershop, a billiard room, and a massive dining hall. It was constructed by town father Louden Mullin, who also built the first school, helped bring in the Denver South Park Railroad, and built the Mullin Opera House.

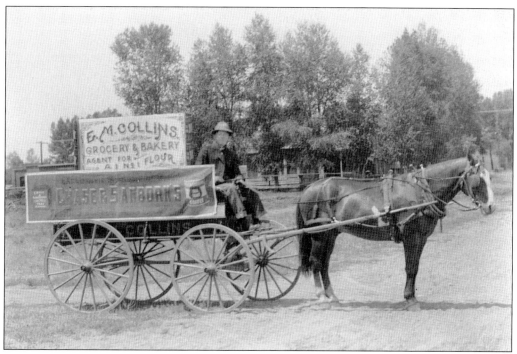

E. M. Collins, Grocery and Bakery Businessman. Collins was one of the first in the grocery and bakery business in the 1880s. Driver Don Summers peddles Collins's wares with an early Chase and Sanborn coffee sign on the side of his wagon.

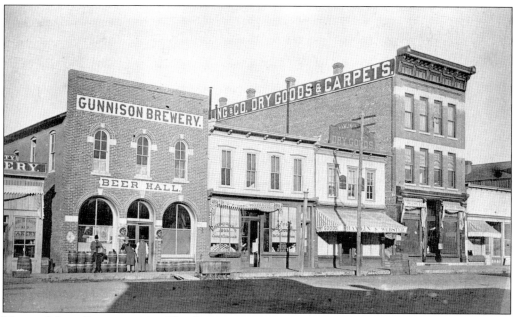

North Main Street, 1882. The Gunnison Brewery was one of several doing a lively business during the boom days. The dry goods and carpets building on the right still stands.

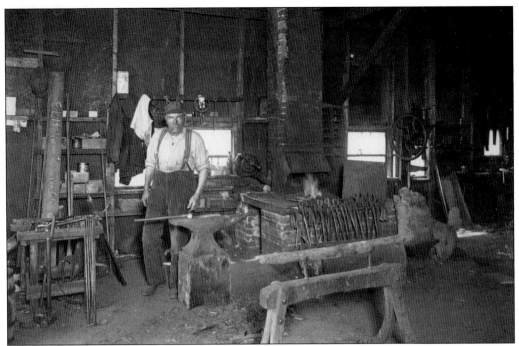

E. L. "Windy" Miller in His Blacksmith Shop. Miller's shop was located in an alley off one of Gunnison's main streets. A good blacksmith was vital in all early mining, railroad, and smelter towns—and Miller was one of the best.

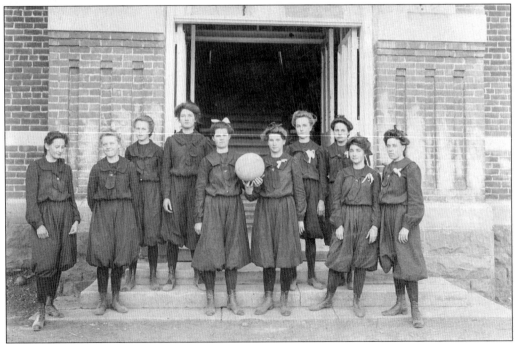

Gunnison Girls Basketball Team. The team appears at the Colorado Street school not long after Dr. James Naismith invented the sport. Little competition existed then, as few other Western Colorado towns had even heard of the new game.

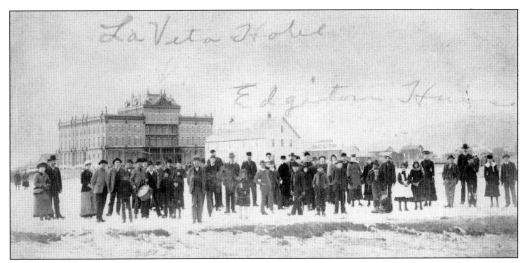

GROUP OF GUNNISON SKATERS, 1888. These skaters are having fun shortly after the building of the La Veta Hotel and Edgerton House, visible in the background. The skating rink was one of the most popular attractions in town and the scene of many festivals.

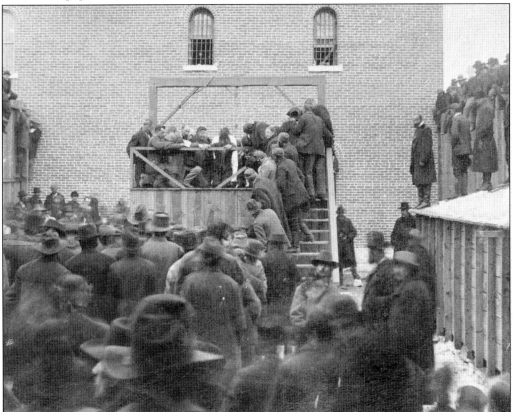

THE HANGING OF THOMAS COLEMAN. In December 1881, Thomas Coleman became the first Gunnison man to be legally hanged. The boss of a Denver South Park Railroad grading crew, Coleman had shot and killed teamster Albert Smith over a gambling debt. A large crowd gathered to watch the execution.

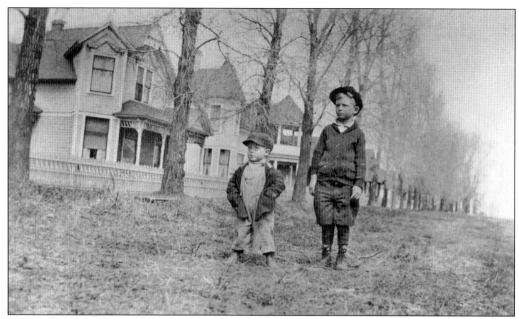

YOUNG BOYS ON SOUTH MAIN STREET, 1890. In this image, Victorian homes have made their appearance, but the street remains grass covered.

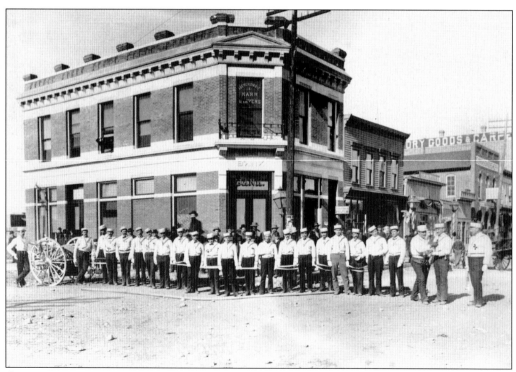

GUNNISON FIRE DEPARTMENT. The men pose in front of the bank on Main Street in 1884. Gunnison had a number of fire and hose companies, all of whom competed with each other on holidays in various contests.

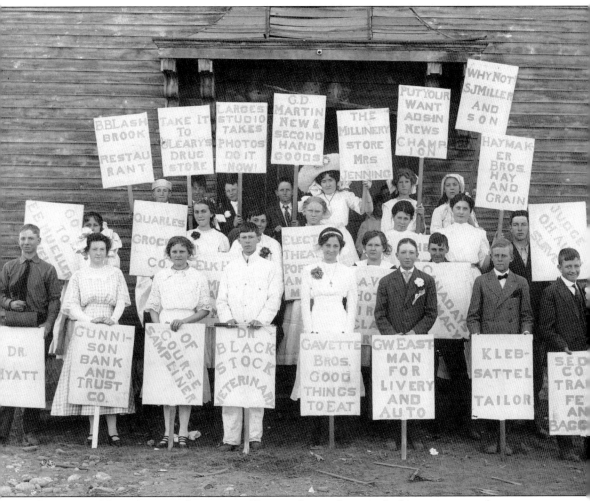

GUNNISON HIGH SCHOOL STUDENTS. Here students advertise for businesses in order to raise money for their graduation. This popular early tradition was very profitable for both students and businesses.

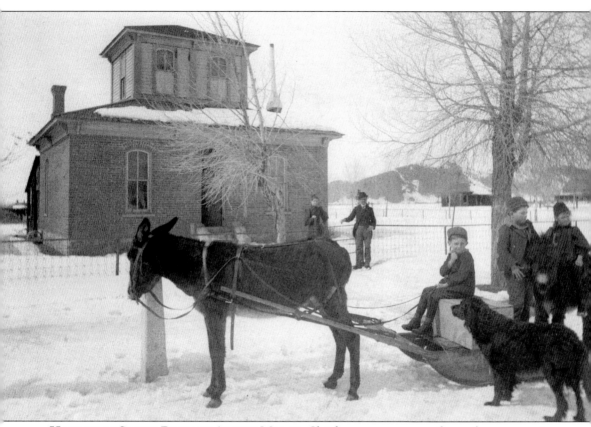

HANDMADE SLEIGH BUILT BY ARCHIE MILLER. Sleighs were a common form of transportation during the bitterly cold and snowy months of winter. Huge sleighs pulled by horses provided winter transportation between Crested Butte and Aspen over the nearly 12,000-foot-high passes.

Two

Jewel of the Elk Mountains

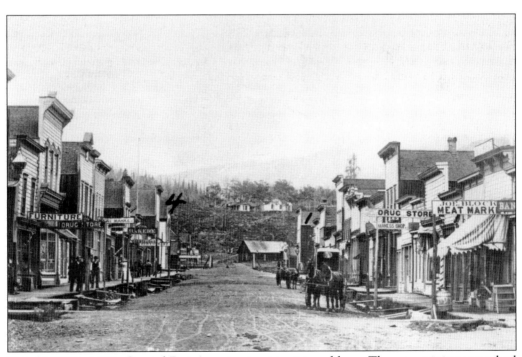

Elk Avenue, 1881. Crested Butte's main street is pictured here. The new mining camp had high hopes of becoming a silver metropolis and a supply town for the many promising camps surrounding it.

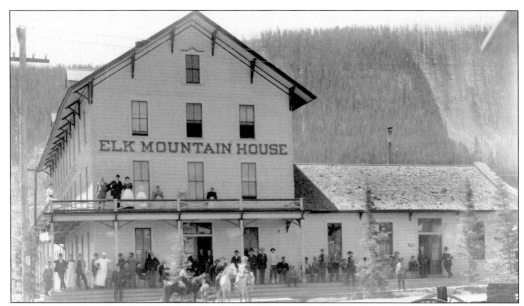

ELK MOUNTAIN HOUSE. This three-story hotel facing the Elk Mountains was built in 1881. An immense stove in the center of the first floor heated the floors above through the use of registers. Other stoves in the corridors of the second and third floors also provided heat during periods of extreme cold.

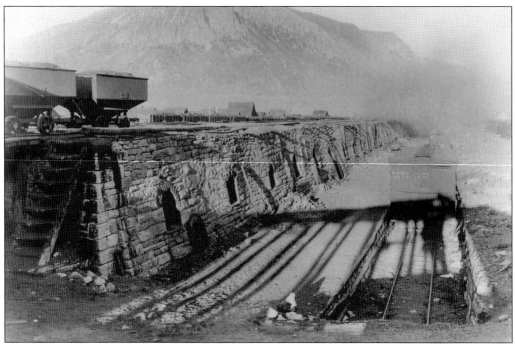

CRESTED BUTTE COKE OVENS, 1884. These 154 ovens were made of fire brick with stone. They were all connected by a large track that ran next to the oven openings, allowing coal to be drawn to them by mule. Coal was baked in the ovens for 48 hours to produce coke. The coke was then loaded on railroad cars and taken to Pueblo, Colorado, where it was used in the production of steel.

CRESTED BUTTE HOUSE. One of the first in town, this hotel opened to serve weary miners. The frame building was rather fancy for the time in a still-to-boom Crested Butte.

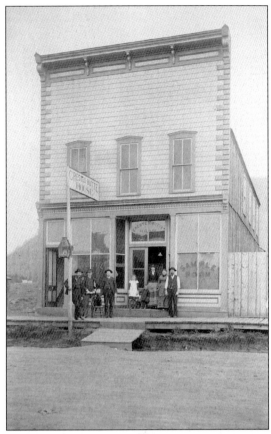

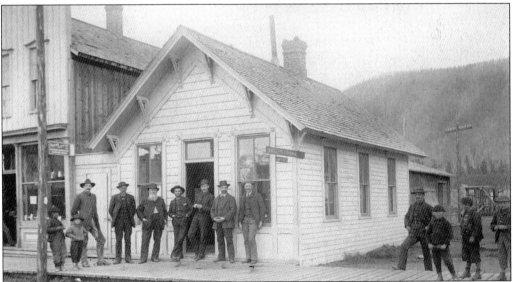

LAW OFFICES OF RICKETTS AND BARNES. This law office began on Elk Avenue in Crested Butte in 1885. In the background of this image is Gibson Ridge, where rich, bituminous coal deposits were found seven years earlier and where daredevil young skiers roared down open ravines on handmade skis.

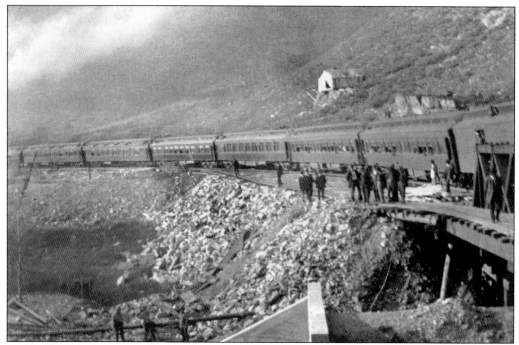

TRAIN OFF THE TRACKS. In May 1884, this Denver and Rio Grande train hit a dynamite charge planted inside a rail a mile south of the Rio Grande depot in Crested Butte. Striking miners were accused of the crime, but there was never any evidence or proof offered to charge them.

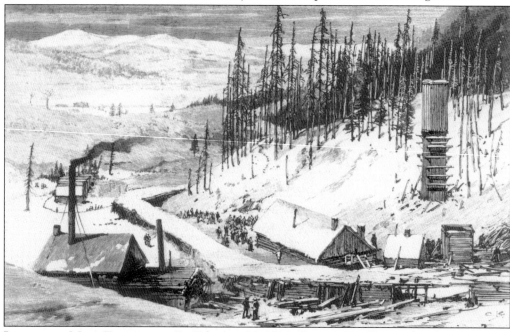

JOKERVILLE MINE EXPLOSION. On February 16, 1884, *Harper's Weekly* ran this drawing of the Jokerville Coal Mine explosion. Seeping methane gas caused the blast, killing 60 miners in one of the worst coal mining disasters in the history of the American West. Forty-six of the miners were buried in a common grave in the Crested Butte cemetery.

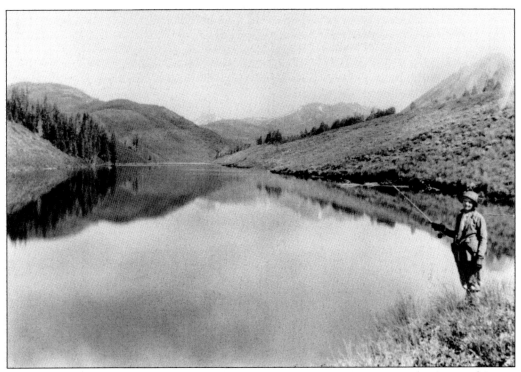

LONG'S LAKE FISHERMAN. A lone fisherman stands next to Long's Lake, north of Crested Butte, in 1890. The lake, now called Meridian, was the scene of boating, swimming, and holiday fun in the town's early days.

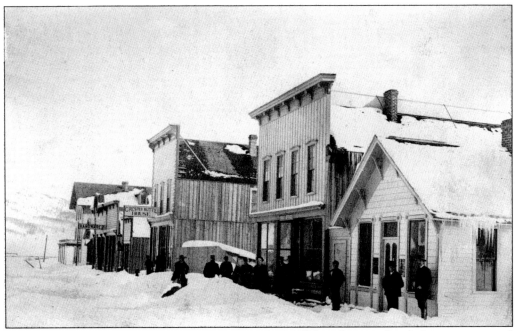

EARLY WINTER SNOW ON ELK AVENUE, 1880s. At 8,885 feet above sea level, the town averaged over 250 inches of snow yearly. As locals were wont to say, "It came early and stayed late."

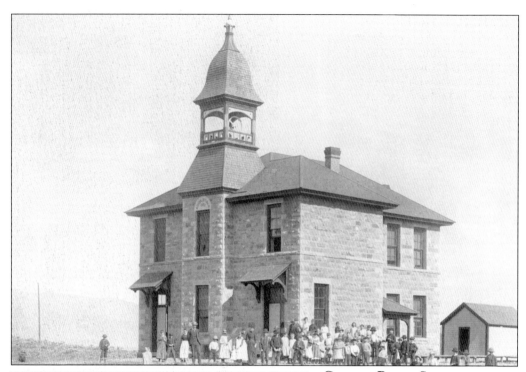

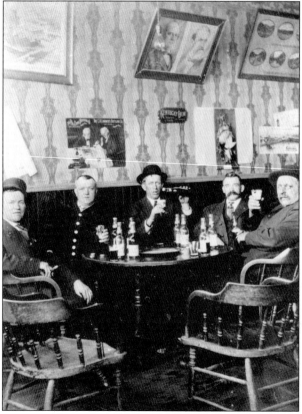

CRESTED BUTTE SCHOOLHOUSE, EARLY 1880S. Early schoolchildren were of Irish, Scottish, English, and Welsh stock. Their fathers, who worked in the mines, were the famed "Cousin Jacks." Beginning in the 1890s, Austrian, Italian, and Slovakian immigrants from southeastern Europe came to Crested Butte and made up the majority of the population.

ROZICH'S SALOON, ELK AVENUE, 1900. This saloon, though one of many, was the most popular during the town's early history. In Crested Butte, it was said by visitors that "the beer was always cold, the polka always fast, and the women all good looking."

CITY HALL IN THE EVENING. Constructed on Elk Avenue in 1883, this building went through many changes throughout the years. Today it serves as an art gallery, bus stop, and cabaret theater.

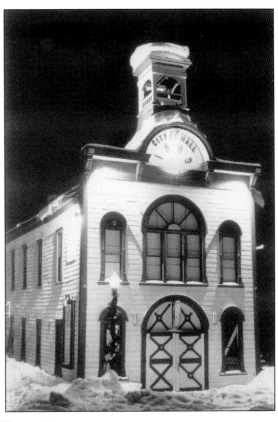

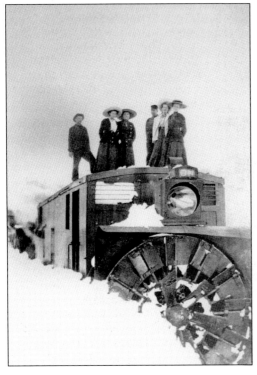

TRAIN BUCKING SNOW. A Denver and Rio Grande Rotary train clears the track between Crested Butte and the coal town of Floesta, 11 miles west. While the train is bogged down in heavy snow, women passengers climb on top of a car to have their photograph taken with some of the crew.

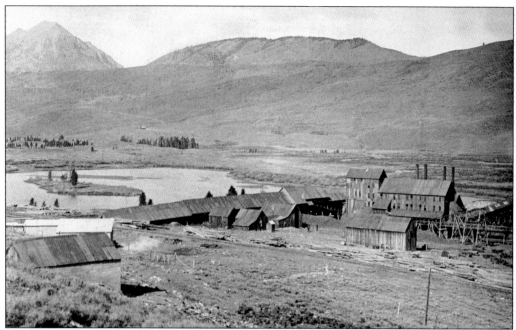

PERSHING ANTHRACITE COAL MINE. Located next to Peanut Lake, a mile north of Crested Butte, this mine opened in 1919 and was named for the World War I hero Gen. "Black Jack" Pershing. During its peak years in the 1920s, the Pershing shipped 40,000 tons of anthracite coal yearly and employed 60 men.

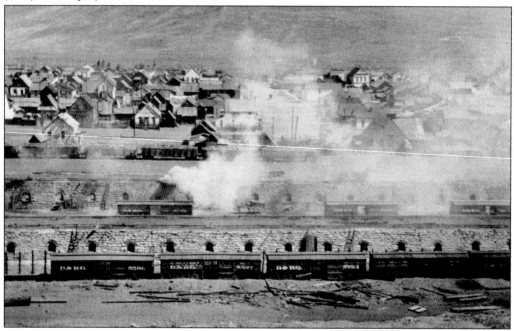

THE DAYS OF PEAK COAL PRODUCTION. Loaded coal cars and some of the Colorado Fuel and Iron Company's coke ovens can be seen here. They are all part of the Big Mine operation. The Big Mine, the greatest in Crested Butte's history, operated from 1894 to 1952 and produced millions of tons of coal.

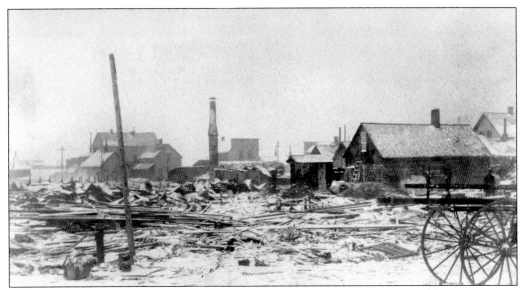

REMAINS OF THE JANUARY 9, 1893, FIRE. This disastrous blaze was one of many that plagued the town. The fire started in the Carlisle and Tetard Market on Elk Avenue and quickly roared out of control, destroying most of the street and causing $40,000 in damage.

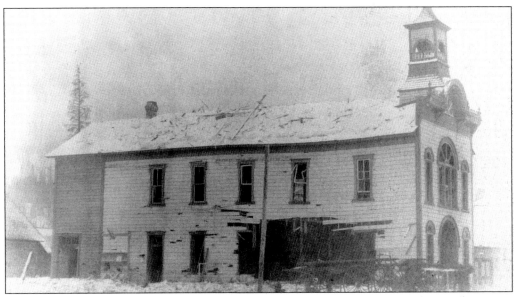

CRESTED BUTTE FIRE HALL AFTER THE 1893 FIRE. In an effort to stop the conflagration, firemen used 50 pounds of giant powder to blow up A. E. Miller's furniture store. They used too much of the explosives, however, and the blast broke every window in town and tore a gaping hole in the side of the hall.

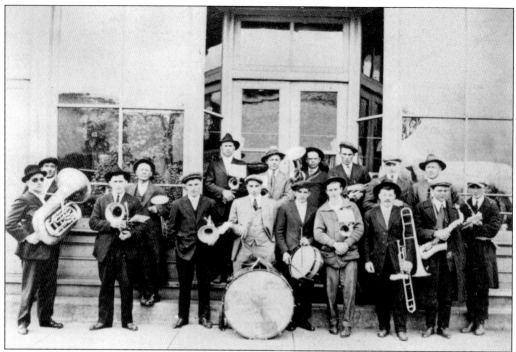

CRESTED BUTTE TOWN BAND, START OF 20TH CENTURY. The people of the town had come from countries in southeastern Europe where folk dancing was prominent. They brought their culture to Crested Butte with dancing every weekend, at weddings, and on holidays. Polkas, waltzes, and schottisches were the dances of choice.

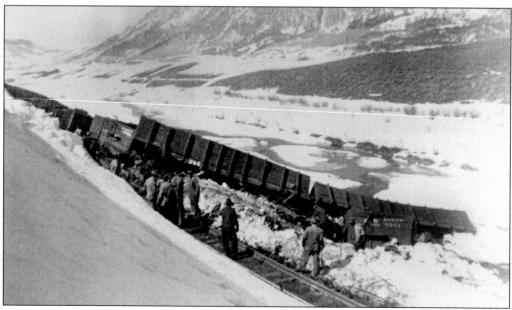

DENVER AND RIO GRANDE COAL TRAIN. Running empty into Crested Butte, this train was knocked from the tracks by a huge avalanche just south of town in 1940. Fortunately, no one was injured, but it took a yeoman effort to get the train back on the tracks.

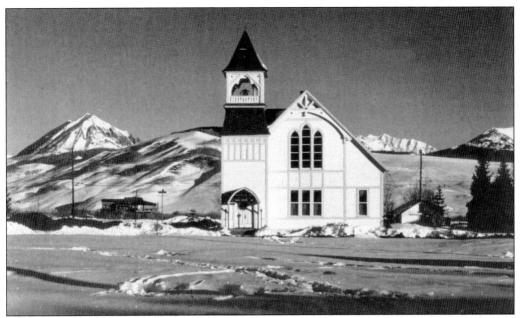

UNION CONGREGATIONAL CHURCH OF CRESTED BUTTE. This beautiful church was built in 1882 as a community worship hall serving all denominations. The following year it became strictly Protestant. In 1917, the bell from the Irwin silver camp's Protestant church was placed in the Union Congregational belfry.

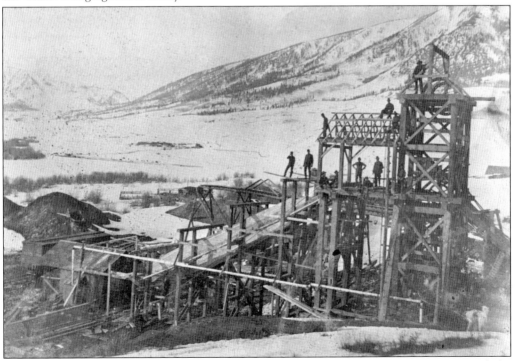

BUILDING THE TIPPLE OF THE BIG MINE. The Colorado Fuel and Iron Company opened the Big Mine in 1894. It was soon producing 1,000 tons of coal a day and employing 400 men. The average wage for the coal miners was $4 per day.

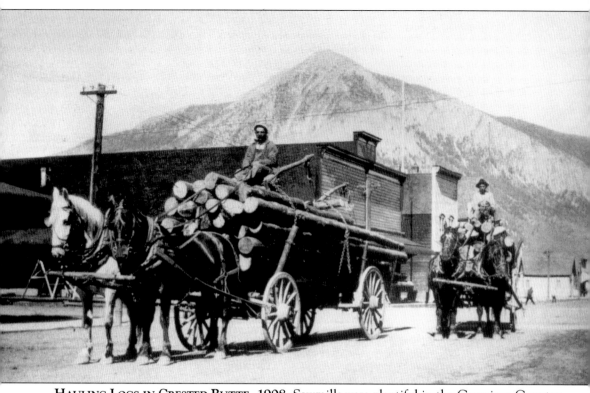

HAULING LOGS IN CRESTED BUTTE, 1908. Sawmills were plentiful in the Gunnison Country because of the great need for railroad ties, mine props, and log cabins. The sawmill operator was one of the most important men in the opening of new mining regions.

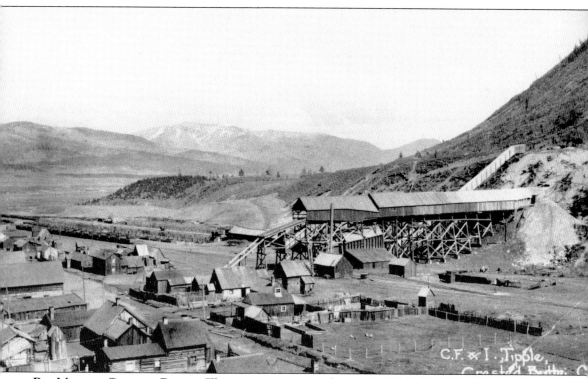

BIG MINE OF CRESTED BUTTE. The mine was at its peak just after 1900. Its 154 coke ovens and railroad tracks are visible here. Between 1894 and 1910, the mine produced 2 million tons of coal and 500,000 tons of coke, and was the third largest coal mine in Colorado. Total trackage in the mine was more than six miles, and 70 mules hauled the product from the vein to waiting coal cars.

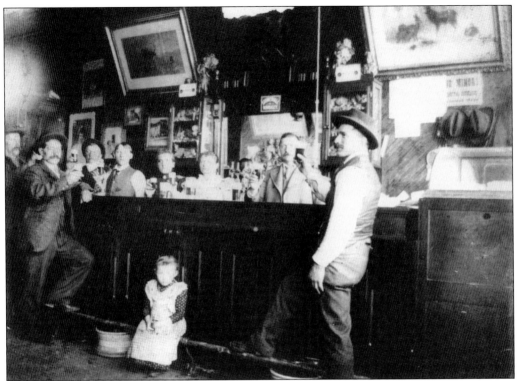

SALOON. After a day of hard work, many coal miners stopped at the saloons to quench their thirst and engage in conversation with their fellow men.

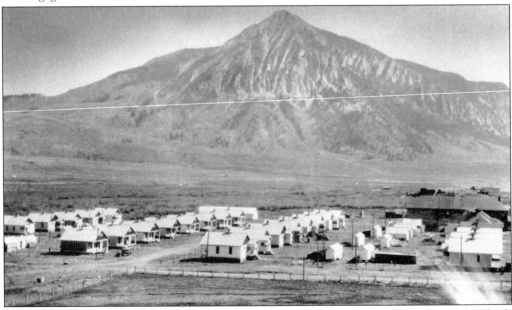

COMPANY HOUSES. These houses were located in a beautiful setting, with the 12,171-foot-high Crested Butte Mountain in the background. The town was dominated by the Colorado Fuel and Iron Company, which provided company housing and a company store where miners and their families purchased most of their goods.

BANK NIGHT AT THE PRINCESS THEATRE, JANUARY 1934. The tremendous amount of snow on Elk Avenue necessitated tunneling to get into businesses. Bank Night started at the Egyptian Theatre in Delta, Colorado, in 1933 to induce people to come to the movies during the Depression. All ticket stubs were put into a barrel, and a winner was drawn just before the feature film. The winner received $80, a tremendous sum on this night in 1934.

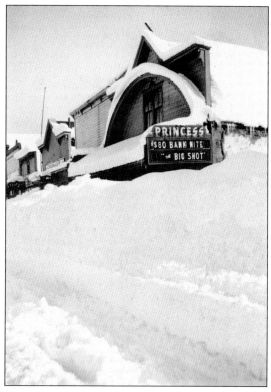

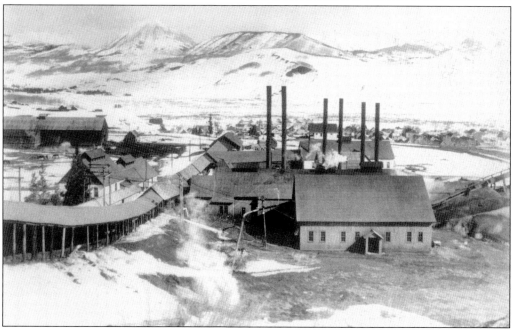

COLORADO FUEL AND IRON COMPANY'S BIG MINE. With headquarters in Pueblo, Colorado, the Colorado Fuel and Iron Company owned dozens of coal mines throughout Colorado, including the Big Mine. This view, taken from the flank of Gibson Ridge, shows the long tipple and mine buildings with Gothic Mountain in the background.

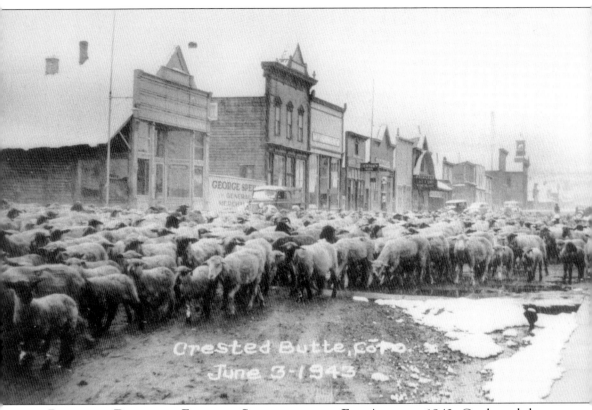

RANCHERS DRIVING A FLOCK OF SHEEP THROUGH ELK AVENUE, 1943. Cattle and sheep competed for the available federal land in the Gunnison Country. After a bitter cattle-sheep war that lasted more than 20 years in the early 20th century, the cattlemen succeeded.

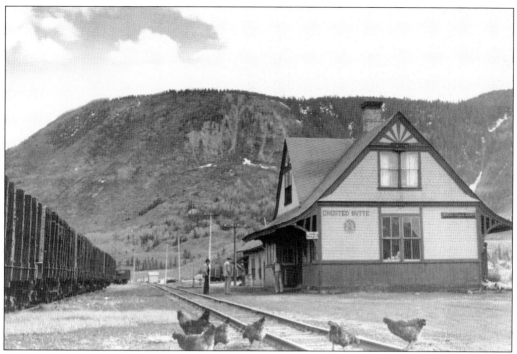

DENVER AND RIO GRANDE RAILROAD DEPOT, 1947. The Denver and Rio Grande Railroad arrived in Crested Butte in November 1881, running tracks 28 miles north out of Gunnison. When the coal mines shut down, the company pulled up its tracks in 1955, ending 74 years of continuous service.

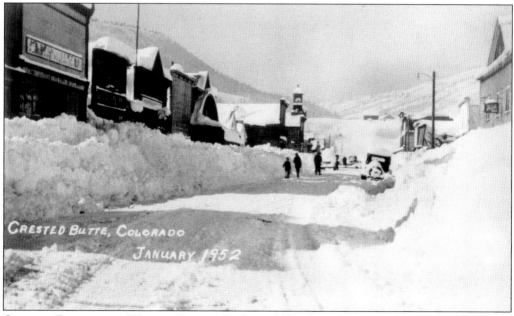

CRESTED BUTTE ON A WINTER DAY, 1952. Snow fell early and often, and because of the town's high elevation, it lingered into May or June. Occasionally vehicles were placed on blocks in garages during the winter months because the roads were not plowed.

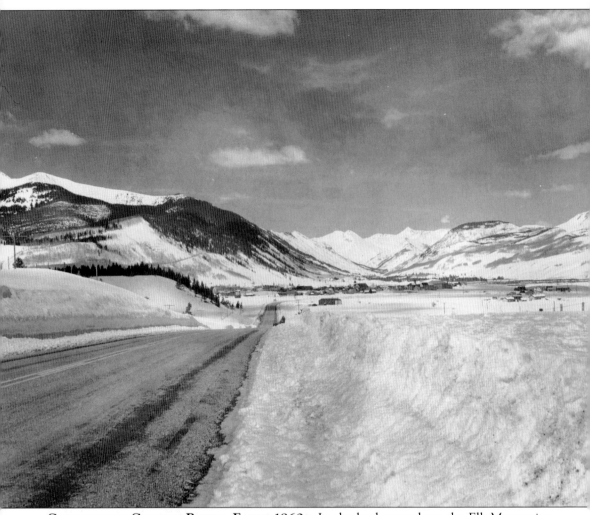

COMING INTO CRESTED BUTTE, EARLY 1960s. In the background are the Elk Mountains, dividing the once-great silver town of Aspen from Crested Butte. The mountain on the left is Mount Emmons, which contains one of the world's great molybdenum deposits. The possible mining of this hardener of steel has created controversy in Crested Butte.

Three
SILVER, HOT SPRINGS, AND GOLD

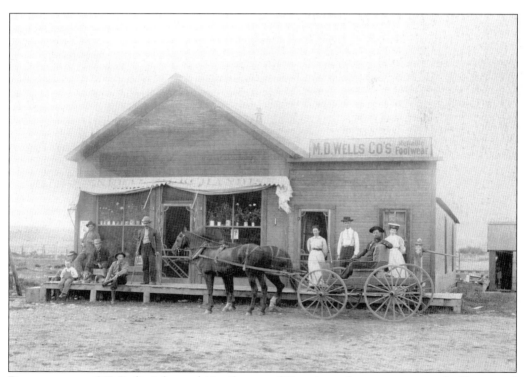

PARLIN ON THE QT. Parlin is located 12 miles east of Gunnison where two streams, the Quartz and Tomichi, join. The QT (Quartz and Tomichi) post office–store still stands. The little agricultural village came into existence when John Parlin started a dairy ranch there. The H. D. Wells Store began in 1880 as one of Parlin's first buildings.

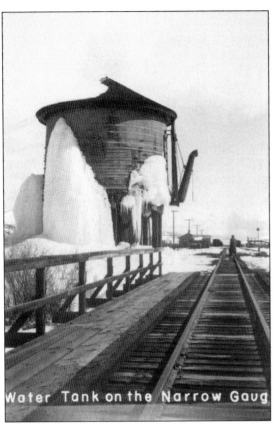

WATER TANK AT PARLIN ON THE NARROW-GAUGE LINE. The Denver and Rio Grande Railroad needed some of rancher John Parlin's land as a right-of-way. Parlin agreed to give the land for free provided trains would stop there for five minutes so he could sell milk to passengers. The railroad agreed, and a handshake sealed the deal.

SHERIDAN SCHOOLHOUSE. Ranch children from around the QT and Parlin attended class at this one-room school, typical of most of the rural schools in the Gunnison Country in the early days. Rarely did one have over 20 students.

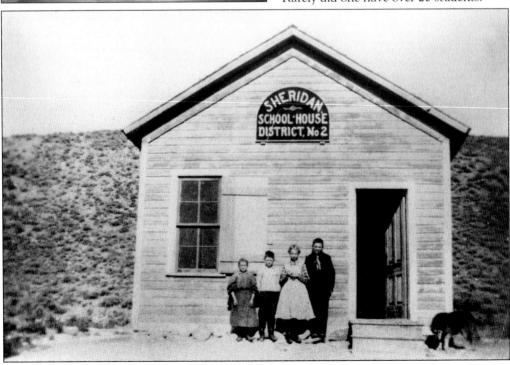

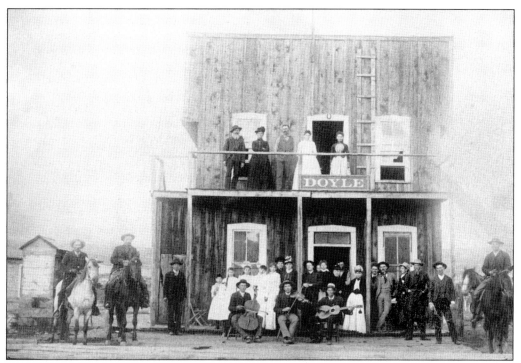

DOYLEVILLE POST OFFICE AND HOTEL. Doyleville began in 1876 when Henry Doyle of Michigan's Upper Peninsula homesteaded 160 acres on Tomichi Creek 17 miles east of Gunnison. The little village became a stop for the Barlow and Sanderson Stageline and then welcomed the arrival of the Denver and Rio Grande Railroad in 1881.

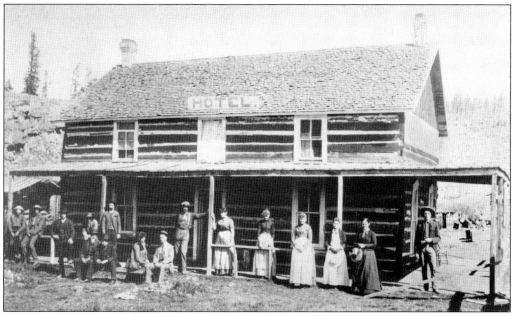

ELGIN HOT SPRINGS HOTEL, 1882. Charles Elgin also built the famed Elgin House, which contained eight bathrooms for guests. The resort became a popular center for individuals seeking cures for rheumatism, arthritis, and other ailments.

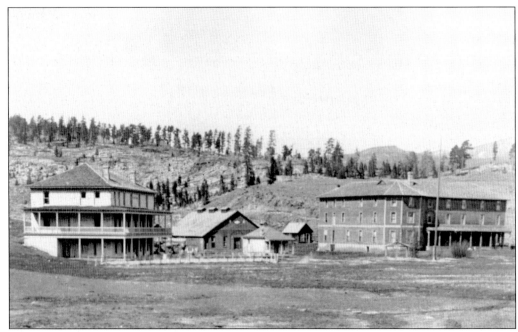

WAUNITA HOT SPRINGS, 1889. The hot springs, located 26 miles southeast of Gunnison, opened in 1879 and, by 1882, included a two-story hotel and a bathhouse. Some 16 springs averaging 160 degrees drew people to this area, which soon added a post office, a restaurant, and a three-story concrete sanitarium and swimming pool. It was a unique experience to swim in the open pool while snow fell and temperatures reached 20 below zero.

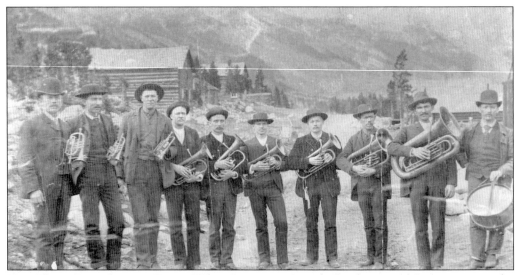

THE WHITE PINE CORNET BAND. White Pine was situated 45 miles east of Gunnison near the head of Tomichi Creek and in the shadows of the 11,312-foot-high Monarch Pass. In the 1880s, it was a thriving silver camp with a population of over 2,000. The cornet band, seen here in 1891, was well known for its music.

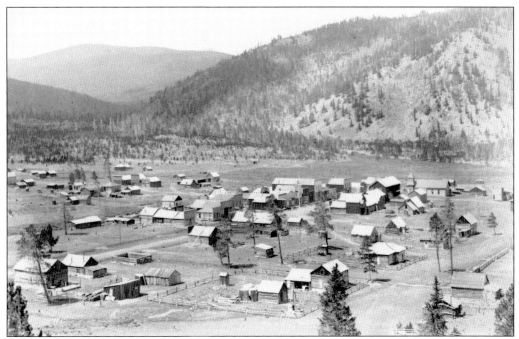

OHIO CITY, 1880S. Gold brought prospectors into a beautiful valley where the Quartz and Gold Creeks came together 19 miles east of Gunnison. Ohio City soon boasted hotels and newspapers, and greeted the arrival of the Denver South Park and Pacific Railroad in 1882.

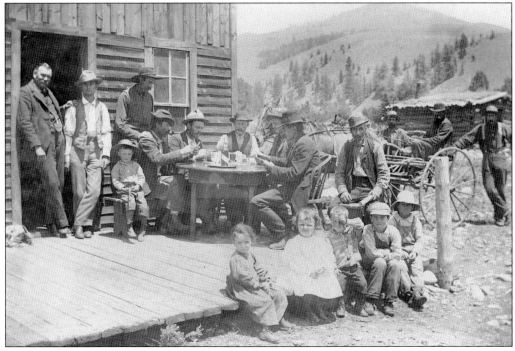

OHIO CITY LOCALS PLAYING POKER. Men engage in friendly competition on their day of rest, a Sunday in 1884. Poker was a common form of entertainment in the early mining camps, with Three-card Monte and Brag as two of the favorite games.

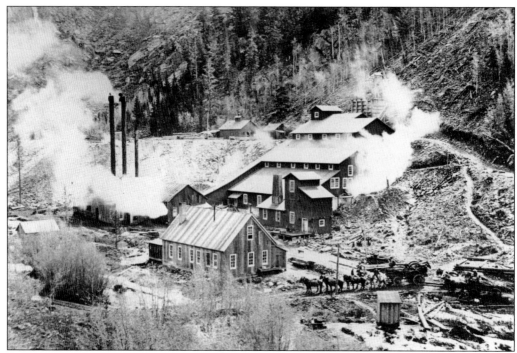

THE FAMED RAYMOND GOLD MINE. This Ohio City mine reached its peak in 1908. Featuring a $50,000 mill that worked night and day, the mine produced over $7 million in gold before closing in 1917.

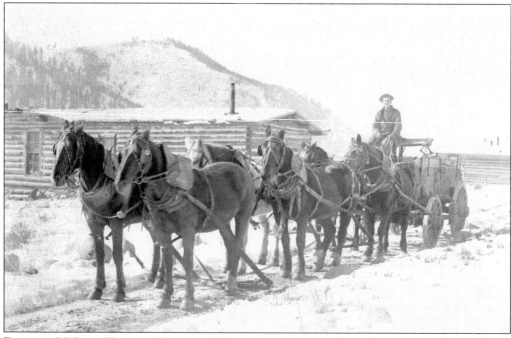

BROWNIE MCLAIN HAULING FREIGHT. McLain's six-horse team hauls freight to the Denver South Park Railroad line in Ohio City in the 1880s. Before the arrival of railroads in the Gunnison Country, the freighter was the most important man in any mining camp.

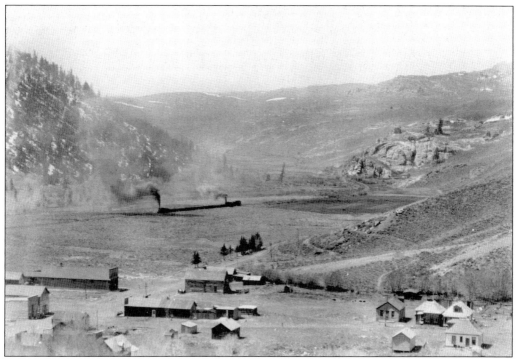

OHIO CITY, 1885. A Denver South Park doubleheader steams out of Ohio City toward the Alpine Tunnel 19 miles to the east. At 11,523 feet above sea level, the tunnel was the highest in the world in the 1880s.

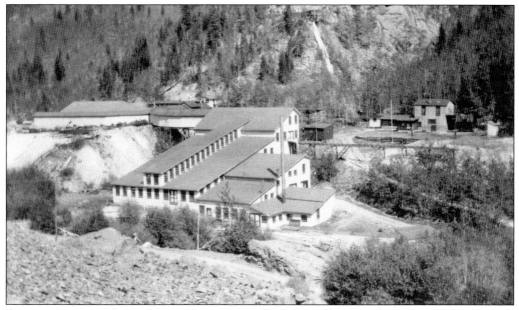

CARTER MILL ON GOLD CREEK NEAR OHIO CITY. Carroll Carter drove a 7,700-foot tunnel, cutting into one gold vein after another, in 1897. He shipped a gold brick worth $3,000 every two weeks. When he retired, Carter told friends he had put $1 million into the mine and had taken $1 million out.

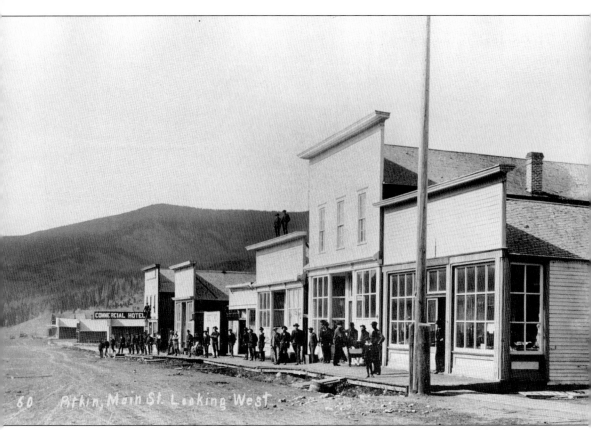

MAIN STREET OF PITKIN, 1880s. Located on Quartz Creek, Pitkin became one of the five major silver camps in the Gunnison Country. The camp's transient population had reached 4,000 by 1882. The other top camps included White Pine, Gothic, Tin Cup, and Irwin. As silver prices continued to plummet, Pitkin's fortunes soon faded.

BILLY REESE'S SALOON, PITKIN, 1881. Billy Reese was one of the top businessmen in the silver camp. Before the arrival of the Denver South Park Railroad in 1882, his beer kegs were brought by wagon from the nearest railroad end of track.

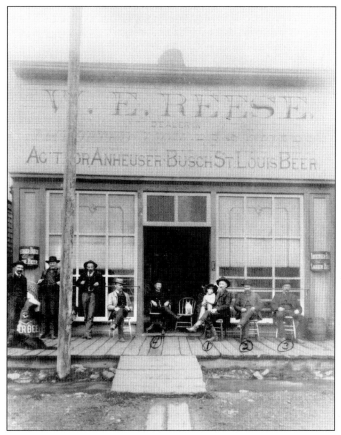

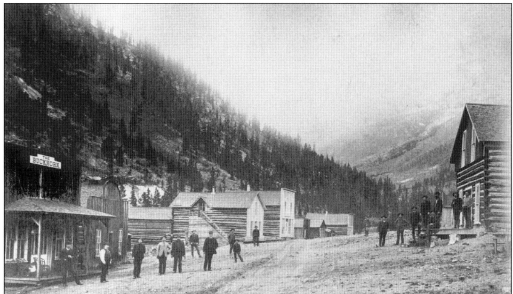

PROMISING SILVER CAMP OF TOMICHI, 1881. Lying near the headwaters of Tomichi Creek and the Continental Divide, by 1882 this camp had 1,500 miners, sawmills, promising mines, a post office, and a bank.

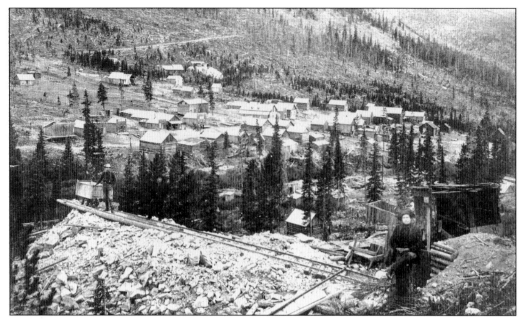

Tomichi during its Heyday, 1880s. Some of the Magna Charta Mine workings can be seen in the foreground. A massive avalanche in March 1884 wiped out all mine buildings and piled snow up to a depth of over 100 feet before coming to a halt in Tomichi Creek.

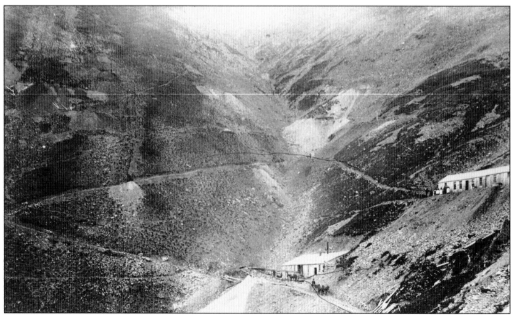

Legal Tender Mine Workings at Tomichi, 1883. The Legal Tender was one of the good-paying mines of the silver camp but was only accessed at a very high elevation by a narrow, steep, and treacherous road that switchbacked continually to the mine.

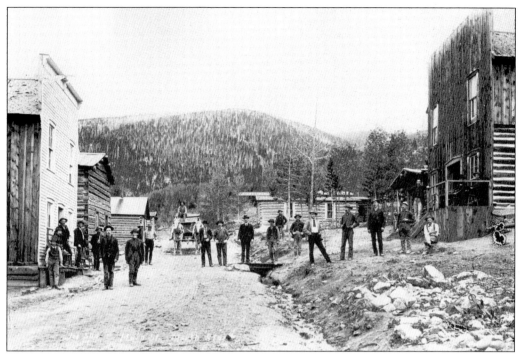

NORTH STAR, 1886. Located above White Pine up Galena Gulch, this silver camp reached a peak population of 100 and consisted of a post office, two boardinghouses, two hotels, a grocery store, and a saloon. The major mine was the May Mazeppa. After a promising first decade, North Star succumbed to the silver panic of 1893.

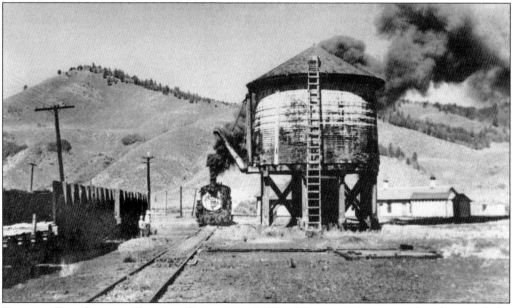

DENVER RIO GRANDE ENGINE, SARGENTS, 1950s. The narrow-gauge railroad entered the Gunnison Country over the 10,856-foot-high Marshall Pass above Sargents in 1881 and opened up the Western Slope of Colorado. During the building of the railroad, there were 14 buildings in Sargents—8 of them saloons!

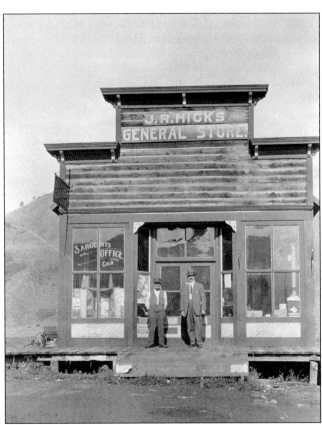

J. R. Hicks General Store, Sargents, 1880s. Sargents was dominated by the Denver and Rio Grande Railroad, which had a roundhouse and turntable, depot, water tank, restaurant, and cattle pens in town. Helper engines were housed at Sargents to assist in pulling huge coal and ore trains over Marshall Pass.

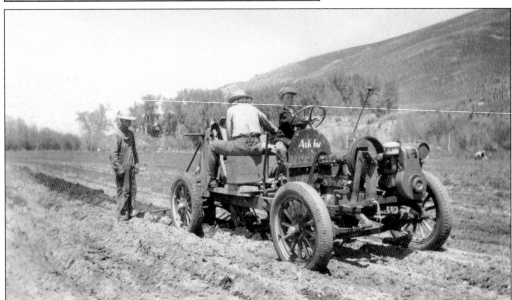

Homemade Strawberry Planter at Sargents. Will Hicks built a one-cylinder air-cooled engine for this machine and used it to power the strawberry planter on his ranch. It seemed impossible that strawberries could be grown in one of the coldest regions in the nation, in an area with a 70-day growing season, but they were.

Four

THE GREAT NORTH COUNTRY

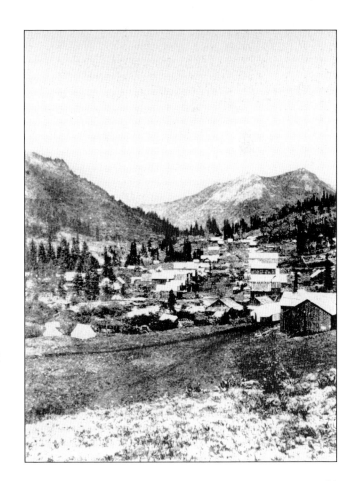

GOTHIC, 1880. Known as "the City of Silver Wires" and beautifully situated where the East River and Copper Creek joined, the camp was named for the 12,625-foot-high mountain resembling a Gothic cathedral that towered over it. After initial discoveries of high-grade silver, Gothic boomed with over 4,000 miners in and around the camp by 1882.

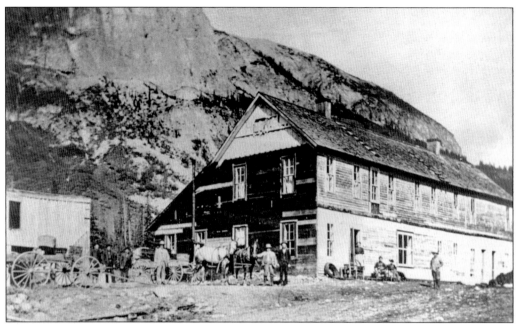

GOTHIC HOTEL, 1881. Built in 1880, this three-story hotel included 40 rooms. It provided low-cost lodging for many of the prospectors who sought their El Dorado in one of the major silver camps of the Gunnison Country.

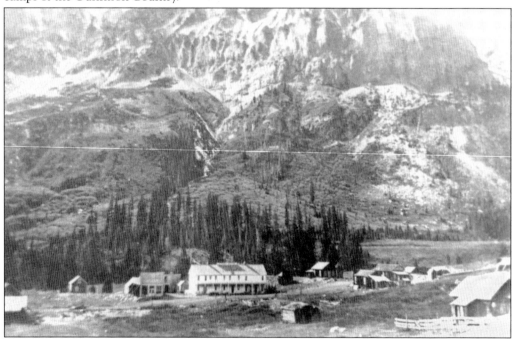

CITY OF SILVER WIRES, 1885. The Gothic Hotel is prominently displayed with Gothic Mountain behind it. The hotel played a big part in the optimism gripping the silver camp in the 1880s. Gothic was the jumping-off point for the 500 to 600 burros who carried supplies into Aspen 25 miles away over the 11,800-foot-high East Maroon Pass. The burros then carried Aspen silver back over the pass to the nearest railroad in Crested Butte.

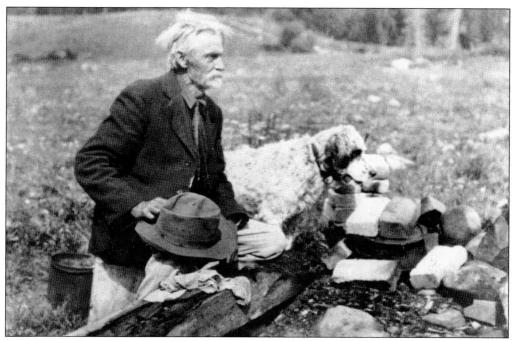

GARWOOD JUDD, "THE MAN WHO STAYED." When Gothic declined after the silver panic, Garwood Judd stayed. He remained in Gothic from 1880 until his death in 1930, serving as self-proclaimed mayor, caretaker, and entertainer of visitors. The Fox Film Company made a documentary on Judd in 1928.

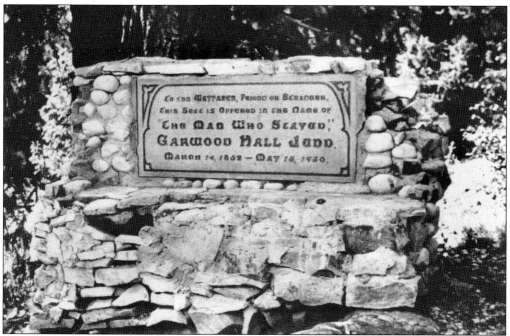

GARWOOD JUDD MONUMENT. One mile up Copper Creek from Gothic is this monument honoring Garwood Judd, who spent 50 years in the once-great silver camp. Judd was a favorite with tourists and schoolchildren whom he regaled with stories about "the good old days."

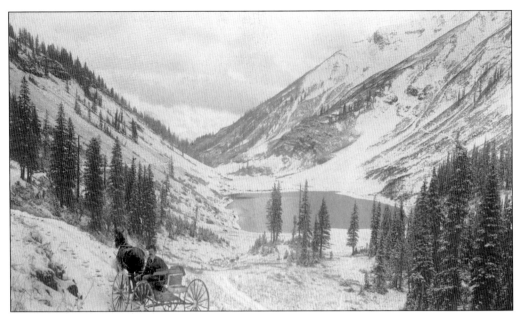

EMERALD LAKE. This beautiful, clear, and deep lake was located on the feared Crystal Canyon road between Crested Butte and Marble. Mountains on both sides of the lake vomited avalanches, making the road one of the most treacherous in Colorado.

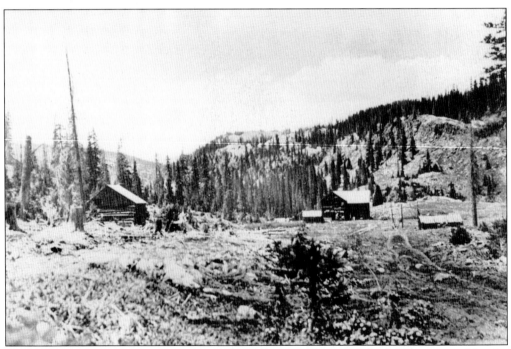

SILVER MINING CAMP OF SCHOFIELD. Although a small camp, Schofield was visited by the Hayden Survey in 1873. This 1890 image shows the camp after its boom had passed. A decade before, Schofield had consisted of 300 residents, two sawmills, four saloons, two stores, a post office, a jail, and the three-story Elk Mountain Hotel.

SCHOFIELD MILL, 1880s. This mill, near the head of Crystal Creek, was important in reducing ores from the Shakespeare, Oxford Belle, Pride of the West, and other mines situated by beautiful Schofield Park.

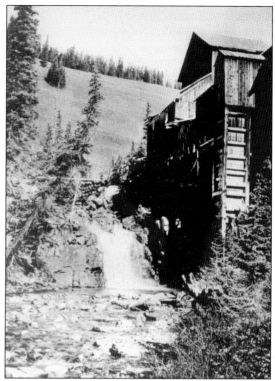

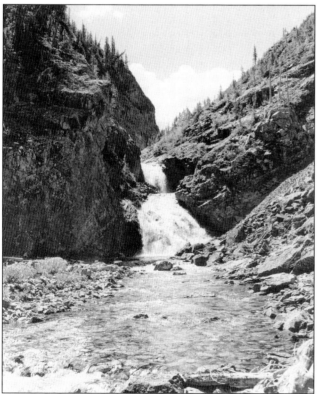

"DEVIL'S PUNCHBOWLS" IN CRYSTAL CANYON. Two huge waterfalls dominate the Crystal Canyon. The canyon road, running above the punchbowls, was constructed in the 1880s and used by freighters and legendary postman Al Johnson, who carried mail between Crystal and Crested Butte year-round. In 1971, nine people died in a one-vehicle accident on the dangerous canyon road near the punchbowls.

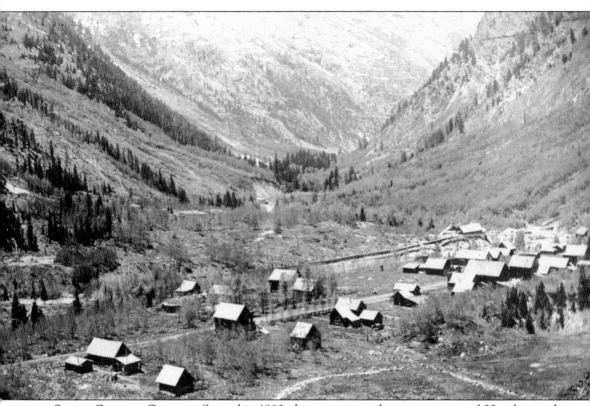

SILVER CAMP OF CRYSTAL. Started in 1880, this promising silver camp operated 20 miles north of Crested Butte near the end of the Crystal Canyon road. The peak population of the town was 600, with the Black Queen being the top mine. From 1880 to 1882, a 100 burro, or "jack," train left the Black Queen every day, packing ore to Crested Butte to the south or Carbondale to the north.

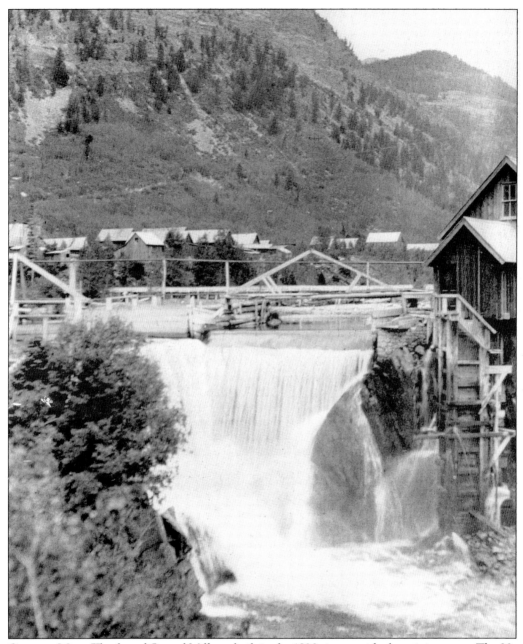

CRYSTAL MILL. The famed Crystal Mill was built in the 1890s just outside the mining camp. The 20-by-50-foot powerhouse overlooked a large dam near the mouth of the Sheep Mountain Tunnel Mine. A turbine waterwheel generated 90 horsepower, which operated an air compressor. The Crystal Mill powered three nearby mines, including the Black Queen and the Sheep Mountain.

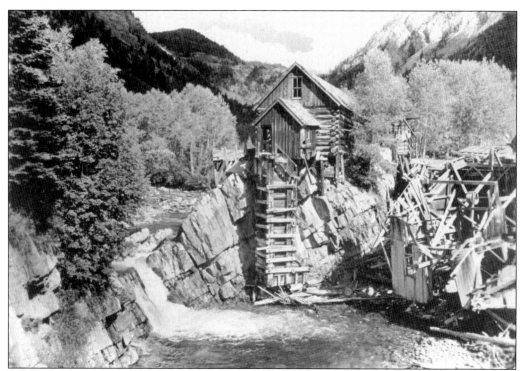

CRYSTAL MILL, 1970S. The mill shut down in 1917 because of hard times in the silver industry. Today the Crystal Mill ranks with the Maroon Bells—two 14,000-foot-high mountains near Aspen—as the most photographed spot in Colorado.

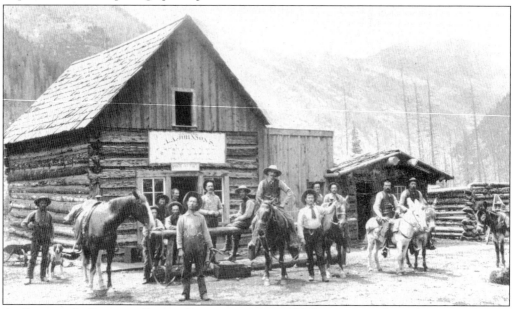

AL JOHNSON'S GENERAL STORE, CRYSTAL, 1880S. Al Johnson came from the St. Laurentian mountain country of Canada to Crystal in search of silver in 1880. Instead of mining, he owned a general store, served as postmaster, and carried mail on the feared Crystal Canyon road over the 10,707-foot-high Schofield Pass on horseback in summer and on skis in the winter.

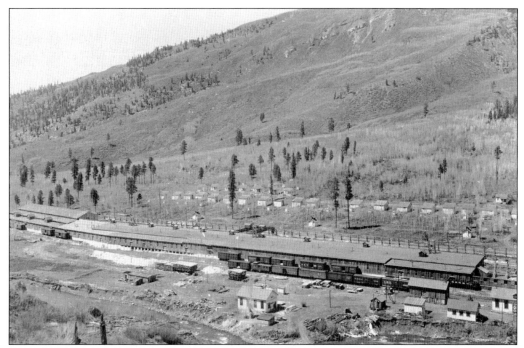

MARBLE FINISHING MILL. The Marble finishing mill, the largest in the world at 1,700 feet long, was located on the Crystal River midway between Crested Butte and Aspen. In 1916, the Colorado Yule Marble Company acquired the contract for the Lincoln Memorial in Washington, D.C., and employed 500 to 1,000 men between the quarries and the mill.

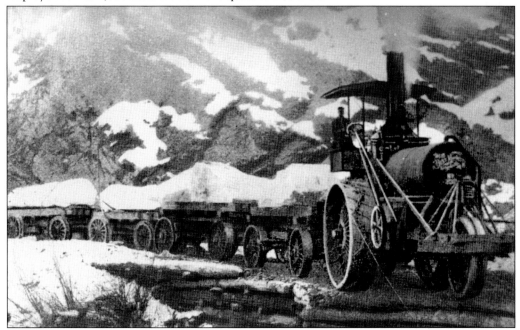

MARBLE'S 110-HORSEPOWER STEAM TRACTOR. This giant tractor, with 8-foot-high steel wheels, had been used to haul timber in California. It pulled four wagons, each carrying 20 tons of marble, down a steep 3.9-mile road from the quarries to the finishing mill below.

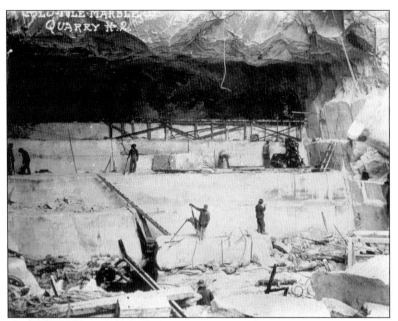

INSIDE A MARBLE QUARRY OPENING. Marble had five different quarries above the town. Whitehouse Mountain contained the highest quality of pure white marble in the world. Many of the Colorado Yule Marble Company workers were Italian, Greek, and Austrian immigrants who lived in shacks in a little settlement near the quarries called Quarrytown.

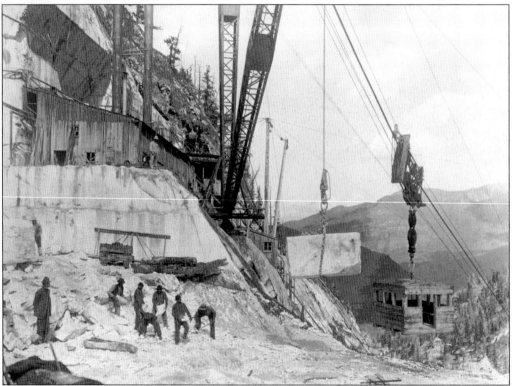

QUARRYING MARBLE IN 1914. Special anchored hoists were used to lift the 20-ton blocks of marble out of the quarries. After 1910, Channing Meek, owner of the Colorado Yule Marble Company, constructed an electric tramway between the quarries and the mill. Although it was faster than the steam tractor, it was also much more dangerous because of the 17-percent grade in sections along the line.

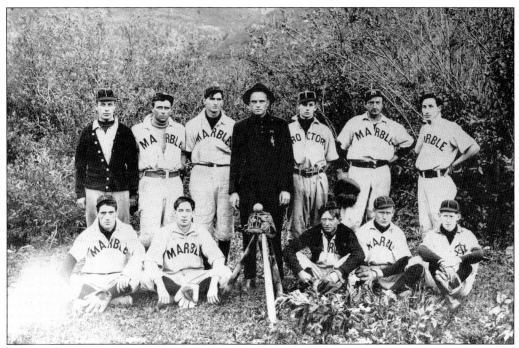

MARBLE BASEBALL TEAM. Marble had one of the top teams in western Colorado, and there was fierce competition with teams from nearby towns like Aspen, Crested Butte, Carbondale, and Glenwood Springs. Much money changed hands after the games.

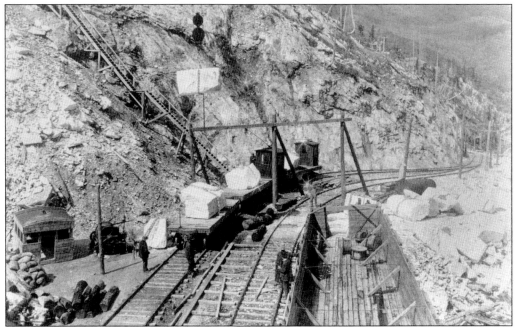

MARBLE BLOCKS TAKEN OUT OF QUARRIES. The 20-ton blocks of marble were loaded on the electric tram for the 3.9-mile trip to the finishing mill. Many accidents occurred throughout the years; in 1912, Marble's main employer, Channing Meek, was killed when the air brakes on a tram car failed.

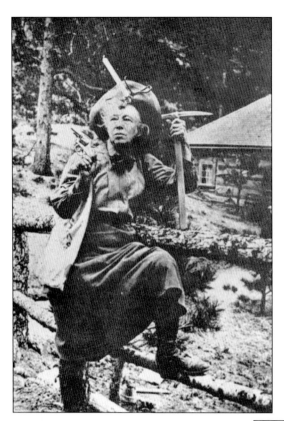

"Captain" Ellen Jack in Crystal. This colorful character claimed to have owned rich mines, engaged in sad love affairs, fought Native Americans, and survived many *Perils of Pauline* adventures in the Gunnison Country. Good with a .44-caliber revolver, she was part owner of the famed Black Queen Mine.

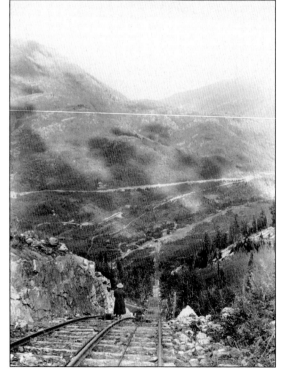

Marble's Electric Tramway. This view looks down from the quarries toward the finishing mill. The entire 3.9-mile distance was very steep, causing newcomers who rode the tram to think they were on a roller coaster ride.

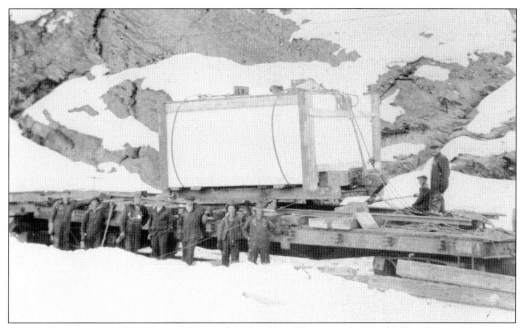

BLOCK OF MARBLE. This huge 124-ton block of marble carved out of Whitehouse Mountain would be used for the Tomb of the Unknown Soldier. It has been loaded onto the electric tramway en route to Marble. Two electric locomotives—one in front of the car carrying the block and the other behind—were tied together to bring the marble down.

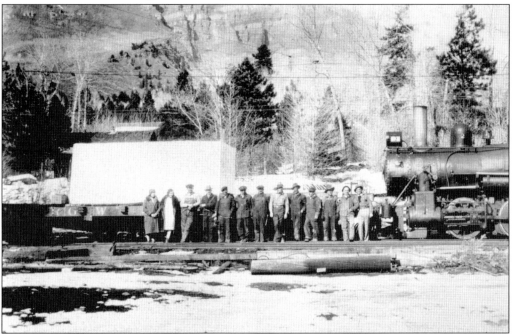

MARBLE FOR THE TOMB OF THE UNKNOWN SOLDIER. The 124-ton block of pure white marble was the largest ever quarried. Transferred from the electric tram to a railroad flatbed in Marble, it was soon on its way to Proctor, Vermont, where the Vermont Marble Company cut it down to 56 tons.

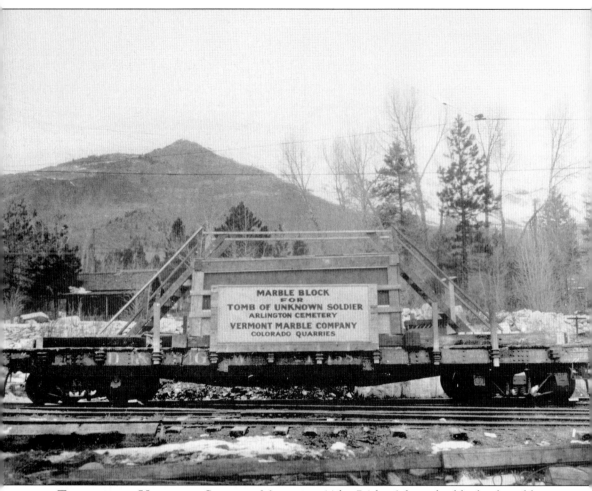

TOMB OF THE UNKNOWN SOLDIER. Measuring 14 by 7.4 by 6 feet, the block of marble was transported by rail to Proctor, Vermont, in 1931. The reduced block was then put in place at Arlington National Cemetery, where it continues to honor the nation's unknown war dead.

Five

LITTLE ENGINES THAT COULD

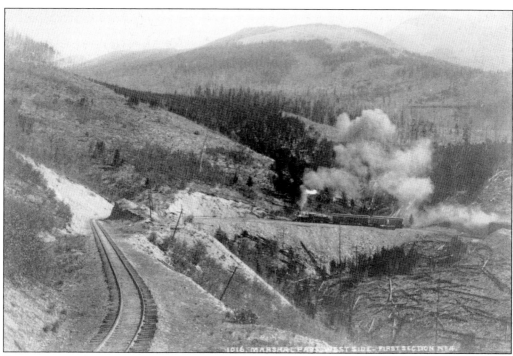

DENVER AND RIO GRANDE TRAIN ON MARSHALL PASS. William Jackson Palmer's Denver and Rio Grande train steams up Marshall Pass, heading west shortly after the pass opened in 1881. Palmer purchased Otto Mears's Marshall Pass Toll Road and used it to get to the Gunnison Country in 1881. The arrival of the Denver and Rio Grande Railroad ensured the success of the mining and cattle industries.

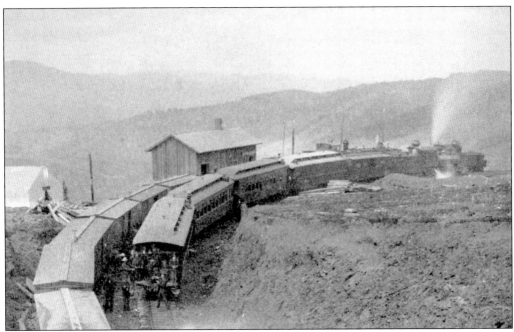

ON TOP OF MARSHALL PASS. The first Denver and Rio Grande train to reach the top of the pass arrived on June 21, 1881. High altitude, driving winds, and below-zero temperatures made working conditions intolerable. Very few men lasted more than a few days laying track on the Marshall Pass line.

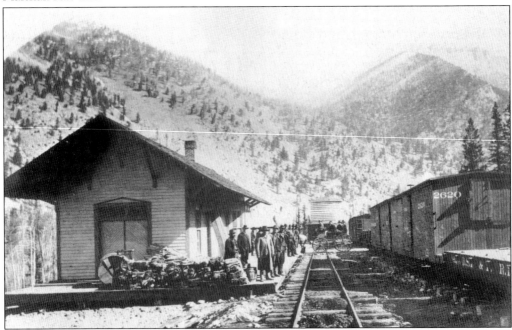

DENVER SOUTH PARK TRAIN AT ALPINE. The Denver and Rio Grande Railroad's competitor for the Gunnison Country was the Denver South Park and Pacific narrow gauge. The railroad was the creation of former governor John Evans. Here the train is stopped at Alpine east of the Continental Divide and not far from the famed Alpine Tunnel.

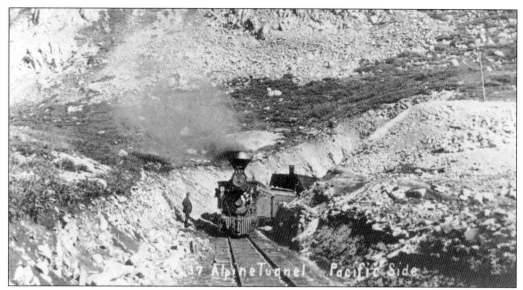

DENVER SOUTH PARK TRAIN EXITING THE ALPINE TUNNEL. The Denver South Park Railroad completed the Alpine Tunnel in 1882. The highest in the world, the tunnel was a marvel of railroad engineering. It was built with a slight apex in the middle to allow drainage out of each end. Some 500,000 feet of California redwood timber were used in the tunnel, along with 1.5 million feet of false timbering. Including approaches on both the west and east ends, the structure measured 2,500 feet and cost $300,000.

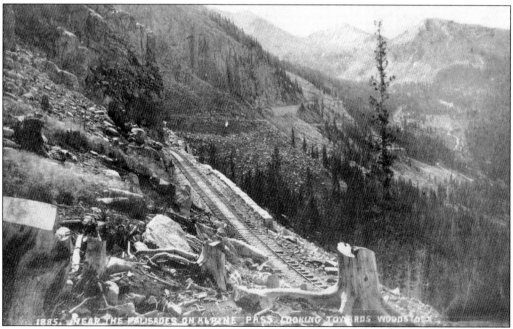

DENVER SOUTH PARK TRACKS ON PALISADES NEAR ALPINE TUNNEL. The tracks ran from the tunnel west to Quartz, Pitkin, Parlin, and then Gunnison in 1882. The palisades were two intricate pieces of rock work on the edges of cliffs designed to keep the road from collapsing. This fantastic feat of engineering was done without mortar. The largest palisade was 450 feet long and 50 feet high.

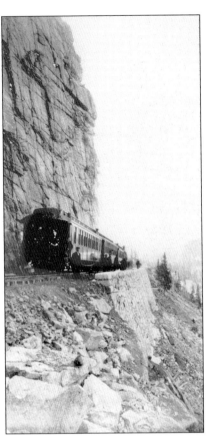

DENVER SOUTH PARK TRAIN DESCENDING FROM ALPINE TUNNEL. The South Park line ran over some of the most dangerous terrain in the Rockies. Long snow sheds were built at both ends of the Alpine Tunnel to keep snow from drifting in. The east portal was guarded by a 16-car passing track called the Atlantic. The west portal had a little camp called Alpine where South Park workers lived. The 10 miles from the Alpine Tunnel to Quartz constituted some of the most sensational track in the United States.

DENVER RIO GRANDE TRAIN IN CRESTED BUTTE. Engine No. 268 sits at the Crested Butte depot in July 1952—only three years before the tracks would be pulled up following the closing of the coal mines. Engine No. 268 is now the centerpiece of the Gunnison Pioneer Museum located at the east entrance of Gunnison.

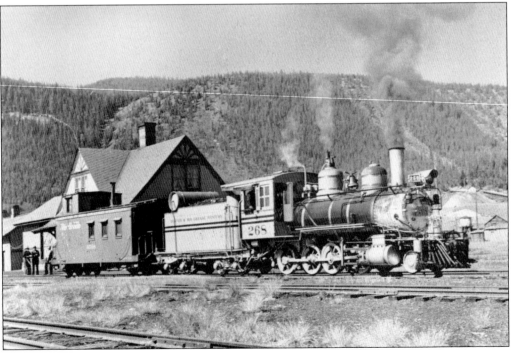

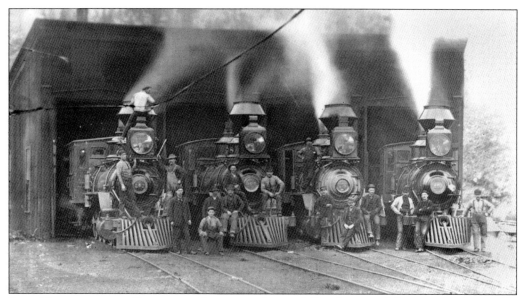

FOUR NARROW-GAUGE ENGINES AT CIMARRON. Located 45 miles west of Gunnison and originally named Cline's Ranch, Cimarron was where the Denver and Rio Grande Railroad climbed out of the Black Canyon and headed west into Montrose over Cierro Summit. Cimarron was home to 250 residents and the Black Canyon Hotel, which served hunters and fishermen. The Denver and Rio Grande maintained the roundhouse and repair shops (shown above) there.

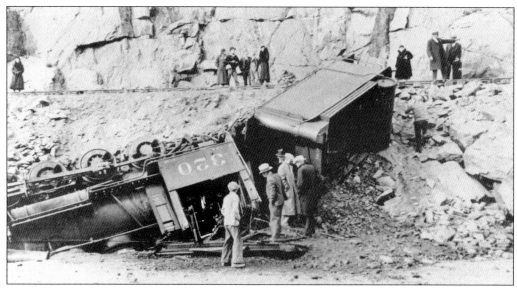

DENVER AND RIO GRANDE WRECK. Engineer Denver "Sap" Richardson was killed in this wreck in the Black Canyon in 1934. The canyon was a railroader's hell because of rock slides, avalanches off the steep walls in the winters, and heavy snow.

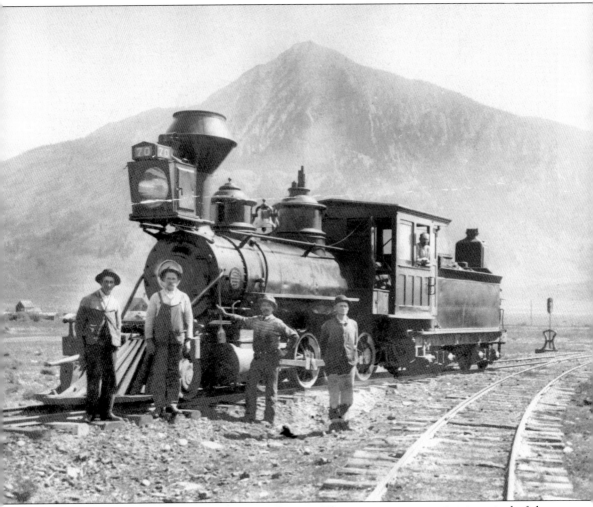

DENVER AND RIO GRANDE IN CRESTED BUTTE. This narrow-gauge engine is typical of those used in the 1880s. In this view, the engine is very near the coke ovens of Crested Butte, preparing for another trip pulling up to 100 coal cars through the East River Valley and Gunnison. Crested Butte Mountain is visible in the background.

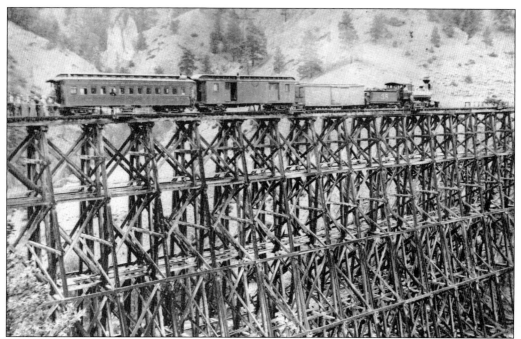

HIGH BRIDGE AT LAKE CITY. About 10 miles north of Lake City, Denver and Rio Grande Railroad engineers had to bridge the Lake Fork of the Gunnison River. The trestle, 113 feet high and 800 feet long, used a million board feet of lumber. It was part of the Lake City Cutoff, a 37-mile branch line from Sapinero to Lake City. The famed high bridge caused those who crossed it to "feel a shiver run up and down their spine."

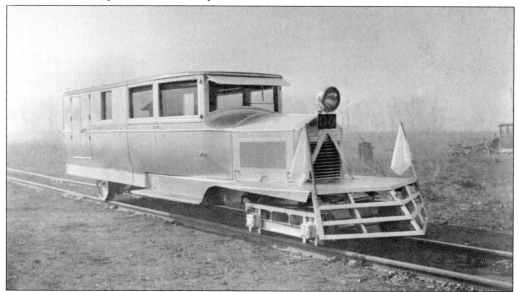

SAN CRISTOBAL RAILROAD. When the Denver and Rio Grande Railroad discontinued service between Sapinero and Lake City on its branch line, the San Cristobal "galloping goose" took over. The brainchild of Lake City mine owner Mike Burke, the San Cristobal carried ore, cattle, and hay for a short time in the 1930s. The engine, seen here, was a Pierce Arrow automobile run by an 80-horsepower Buick motor.

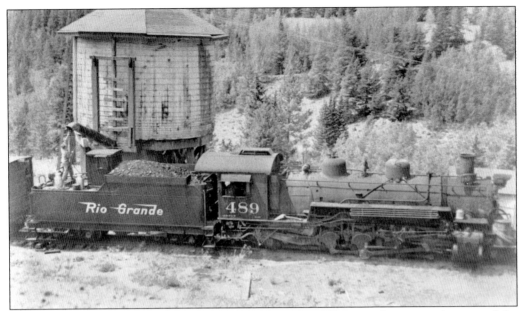

DENVER AND RIO GRANDE TRAIN ON MARSHALL PASS. This train has stopped at one of the many stations on Marshall Pass in 1939. The Marshall Pass section of the railroad ran from Poncha Springs on the east side of the Continental Divide to Sargents on the west. From there, it was only 32 miles to Gunnison.

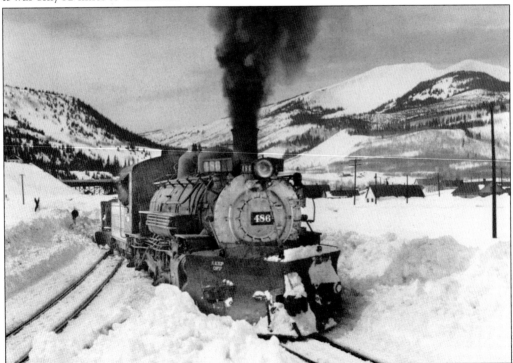

NARROW GAUGE NEAR THE BIG MINE. A Rio Grande engine is pictured in Crested Butte in 1952. In the background are Mount Emmons and its famed Red Lady Basin. The Big Mine shut down in 1952, causing Crested Butte's population to drop dramatically to near–ghost town status.

WOODSTOCK, NEAR THE ALPINE TUNNEL. Woodstock was located four miles west of the Alpine Tunnel on the South Park Railroad line. By 1882, it had become a small railroad town of 10 mining cabins, a restaurant, a boardinghouse, and a saloon. In addition, the South Park Railroad built a section house, telegraph shack, and water tank there. On March 10, 1884, an avalanche smashed into Woodstock, killing 13 people. The town was never rebuilt.

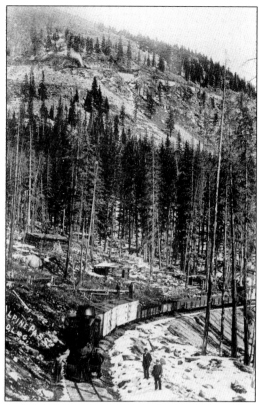

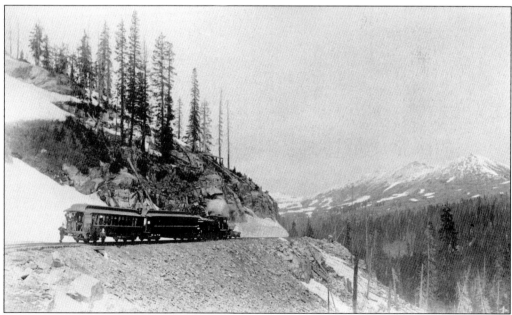

SOUTH PARK PASSENGER TRAIN NEAR THE PALISADES. The Denver South Park Railroad line from Quartz 10 miles east to the Alpine Tunnel passed through some of the most demanding terrain in the mountains. Steep grades, 1,000-foot drop-offs, sharp curves, and heavy snows greeted some of the greatest engineers in mountain railroad history.

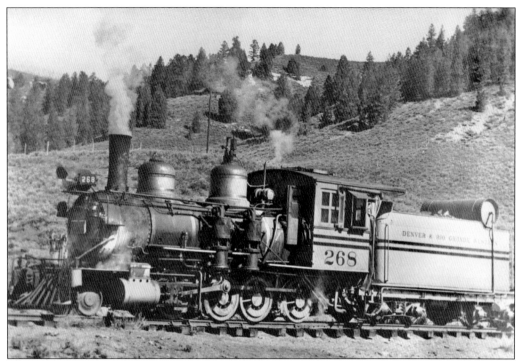

No. 268 on Marshall Pass. In this photograph, historic Denver and Rio Grande Railroad engine no. 268 helps tear up the rails on the line in 1955. Declining traffic because of the closing of coal mines—plus competition from trucks, buses, and airplanes—led to the demise of the railroad.

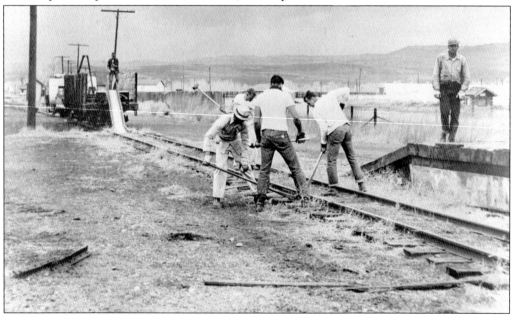

Pulling up Tracks in Gunnison. Western State College football players were among those hired by the Denver and Rio Grande Railroad to pull up railroad tracks in the Gunnison Country in 1955. Here workers dig up tracks in Gunnison while being overseen by Paul Brinkerhoff of Salida (right).

Six

Ski Country

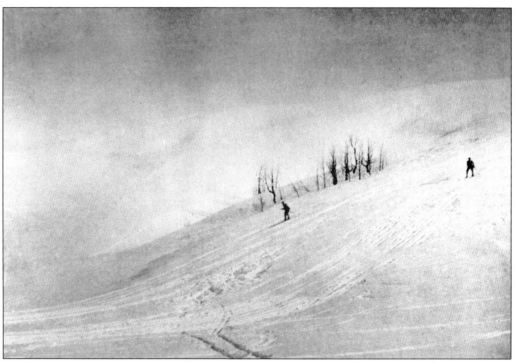

Skiing near Irwin, 1883. Every man, woman, and child had to learn to ski if they wished to get anywhere in the winter in the early mining days. Miners from Canada and Norway helped make the skis and gave instruction. The skis were between 9 and 14 feet long and included a leather toe piece and a heel block. Though crude and handmade, they worked. Soon ski races between mining camps were held on weekends with camp pride and money on the line.

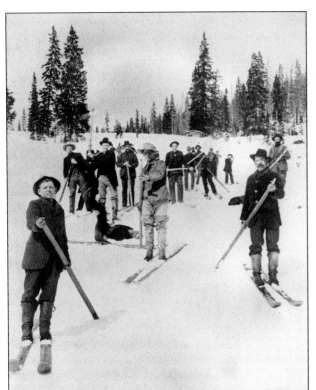

IRWIN AND CRESTED BUTTE SNOWSHOERS, MARCH 1883. Skiers were called snowshoers in the early Colorado mining camps. What we call snowshoes today were then called Canadian webs. Here one can get a sense of the length of the skis and the size of the guide poles used. In the foreground on the left is a teenage Charlie Baney of Crested Butte, one of the greatest skiers in Gunnison Country history and the winner of many tour races.

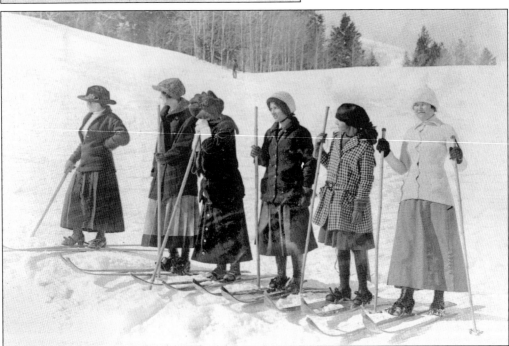

WOMEN SKIERS NEAR MONARCH PASS, 1920S. These six women skiers near the present-day Monarch Ski Area reflect the coming change in equipment. The woman on the right uses two ski poles with baskets on the bottom instead of the guide poles employed by the other women.

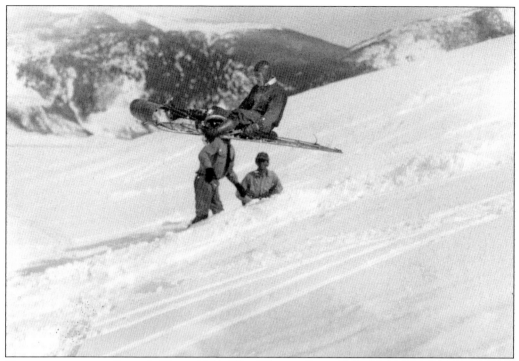

TOBOGGANING AT QUICK'S HILL, 1932. The Western State College Hiking and Outing Club used Quick's Hill, eight miles south of Crested Butte, as a winter playground. All skiers and tobogganers had to walk to the top of the hill for their runs. Here Ernest Miller hits a jump at about 30 miles per hour.

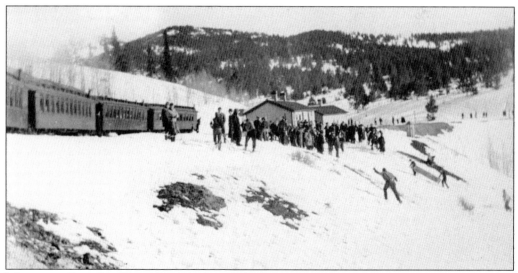

MARSHALL PASS SKI TRAIN, 1938. The Marshall Pass ski train was a special all-day excursion run by the Denver and Rio Grande Railroad from Salida on the Eastern Slope and Gunnison on the Western Slope to the top of Marshall Pass. Over 500 skiers paid for the excursion and skied from the top of the pass to switches below. They were then taken back to the top by railroad for 10¢.

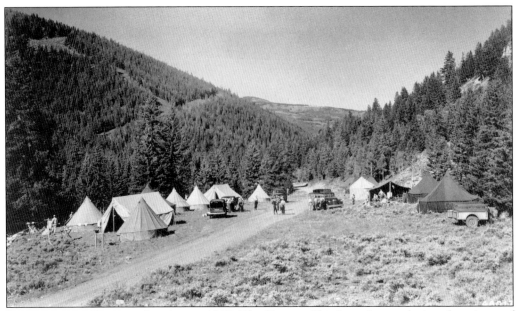

BUILDING THE PIONEER SKI AREA, 1939. The Pioneer Ski Area, begun during the winter of 1939–1940, had Colorado's first chair lift. Local residents of Gunnison built the ski lift with materials from the abandoned Blistered Horn Mine near Cumberland Pass. In this image, worker tents are set up near the bottom of the ski area in the fall of 1939.

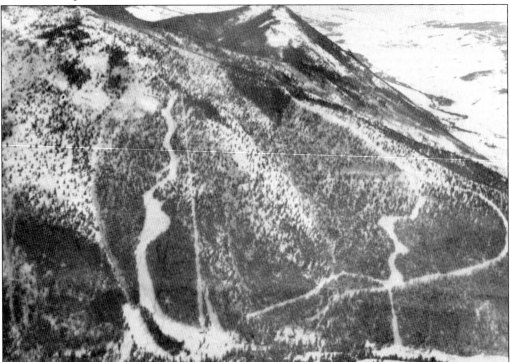

PIONEER SKI AREA. One of Colorado's earliest ski areas, Pioneer was located on Cement Creek eight miles south of Crested Butte. The two main trails were the Milky Way and the Big Dipper. Major college ski races were held at Pioneer, which remained open for a decade.

ROZMAN HILL SKI AREA. Named for John Rozman, on whose ranch it was located during the winter of 1950–1951, this ski area replaced Pioneer. Rozman Hill included a rope tow for a lift and a ski jump used in collegiate competition.

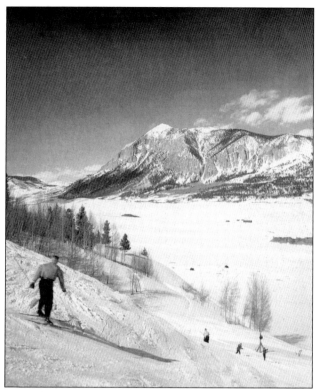

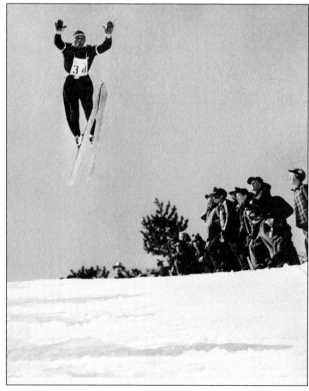

STEVE RIESCHL ON ROZMAN HILL. Western State College ski jumper Steve Rieschl jumps at Rozman Hill in the 1950s. Following his graduation, Rieschl competed in ski flying competitions all over the world. His longest jump nearly reached 400 feet.

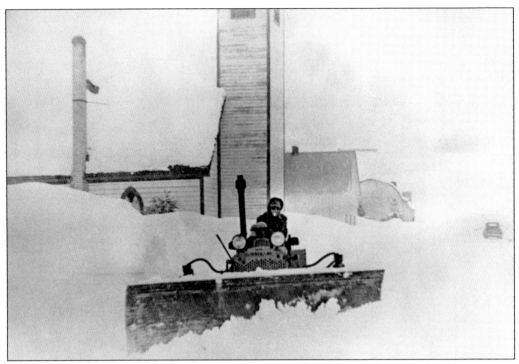

CLEARING SNOW AT CRESTED BUTTE. The winter of 1961–1962 was a fierce one in Crested Butte. Here a snowplow attempts to clear a street after a heavy snow in January. St. Patrick's Catholic Church appears in the background.

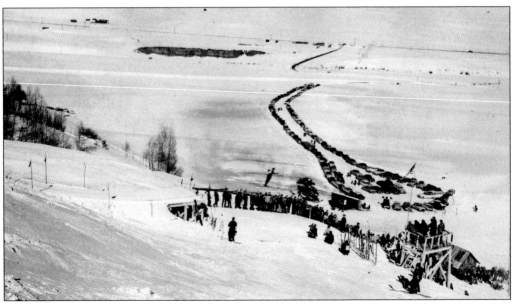

COLLEGIATE SKIING AT ROZMAN HILL. A line of cars stretches from Highway 135 to the Rozman Hill Ski Area, forming a long parking lot during a collegiate jumping and skiing competition in 1957.

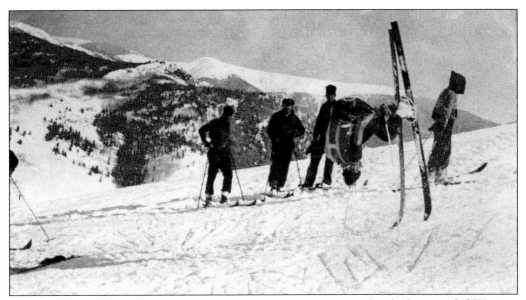

KARL EASTERLY ON QUICK'S HILL. Karl Easterly was a Gunnison local who attended Western State College. In 1938, he learned how to do back flips on skis at Quick's Hill. This occurred nearly a decade before Stein Erickson would make them famous in Aspen. Easterly became legendary in the West with his exhibitions well into the 1950s.

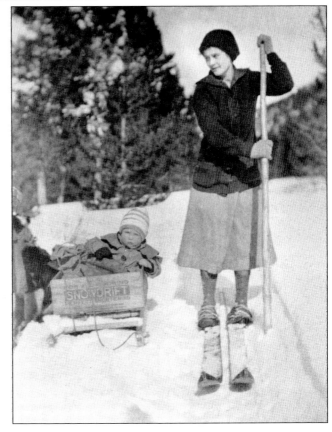

EARLY SKIING IN THE GUNNISON COUNTRY. This young woman prepares to ski from White Pine to Sargents, a distance of 13 miles, in the 1930s. Her son is along for the ride, snuggled in a Snowdrift box atop a sled.

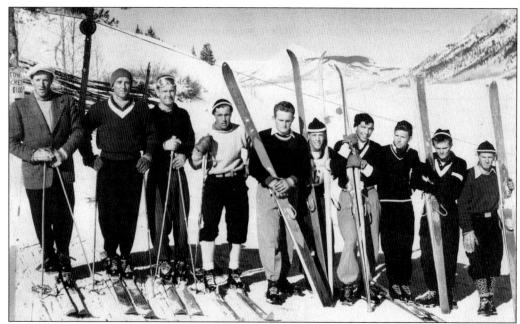

SKI TEAM AT ROZMAN HILL. Western State College ski jumpers are pictured at Rozman Hill in 1952. On the left is Sven Wiik, two-time United States Olympic coach, as well as the college coach. Just behind Wiik is a sign advertising "tow tickets: $1.00."

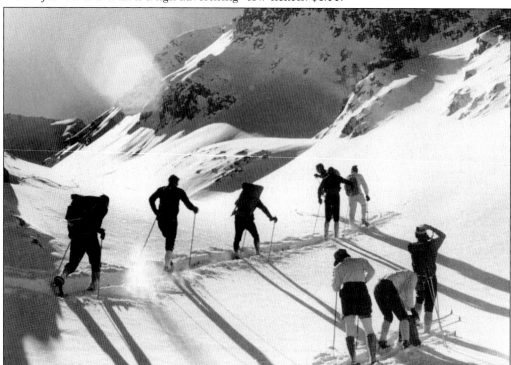

MAROON PASS SKIERS. Gunnison and Western State College skiers approach the top of East Maroon Pass, nearly 12,000 feet high, in 1962. They are en route to Aspen and a great meal at the Red Onion.

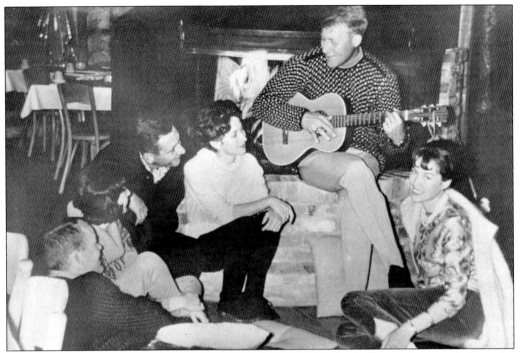

FOUNDER OF CRESTED BUTTE SKI AREA. Dick Eflin, who skied all over Europe while in the military, visited Crested Butte following his discharge. He found Crested Butte Mountain similar to many of the great European mountains and started a new ski area in 1961. Here he plays the guitar during the winter of 1961–1962 at one of the early lodges.

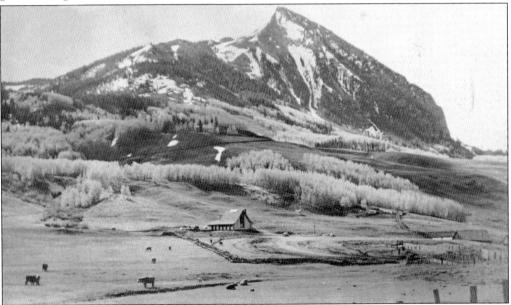

SKI AREA BEGINNING. The Crested Butte Ski Area began in 1961 when Dick Eflin and Fred Rice purchased the Malensek Ranch below Crested Butte Mountain. In this view, cows are still grazing on the ranch with the mountain in the background. A newly constructed warming house, ready to serve skiers, is also visible.

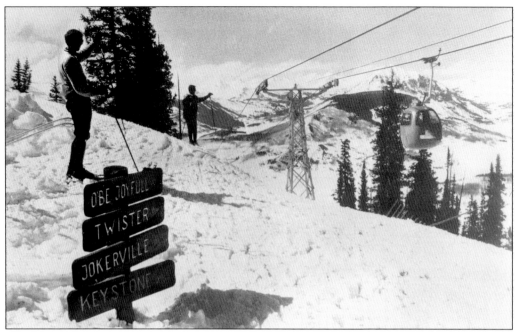

GONDOLA AT CRESTED BUTTE. At the top of the Crested Butte Ski Area, skiers are ready to experience the O Be Joyful, Twister, Jokerville, and Keystone runs. The gondola lift came from Italy and could hold three skiers. It started operating in 1963 but was unable to handle many skiers efficiently.

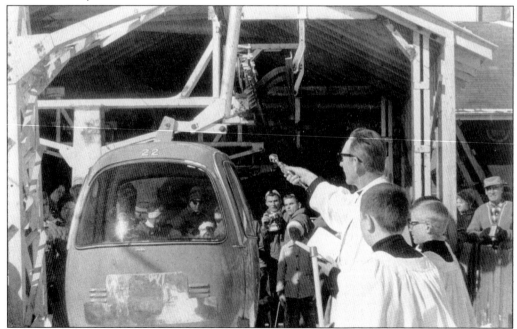

BLESSING OF THE GONDOLA. When the gondola opened at the Crested Butte Ski Area in 1963, tradition dictated that a blessing take place. Father McKenna, a Catholic priest from Gunnison, blessed the gondola, which promptly broke down for the rest of the day. A further indignity occurred when Father McKenna slipped in the parking lot while leaving and fractured his ankle.

Seven
OF MINES AND MEN

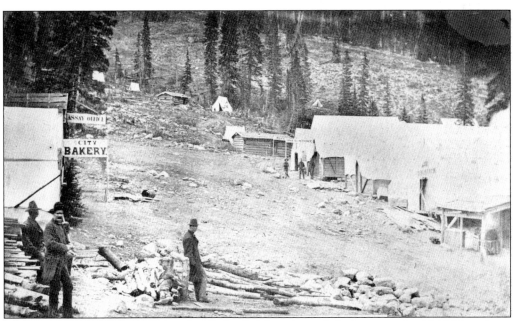

START OF IRWIN. Irwin was located up Ruby Gulch and near Lake Brennand at 10,000 feet above sea level in 1879, following rich silver discoveries. Over 40 feet of snow fell on the camp during the winter, delaying entry until June. By the fall of 1880, however, Irwin had progressed from a tent camp to a town of 529 houses.

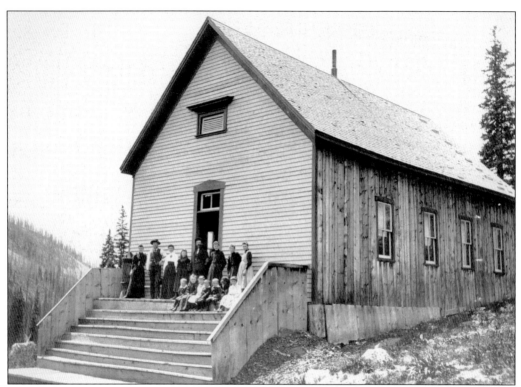

IRWIN SCHOOLHOUSE. As Irwin boomed, tents were replaced with cabins, and soon cabins gave way to frame buildings. The Irwin schoolhouse was built in 1882, eventually serving more than 50 students in its one room.

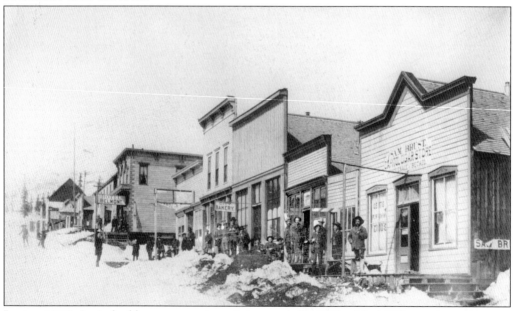

IRWIN, 1885. Irwin had become a major mining camp by 1885, with 4,000 transient miners in town and in the surrounding gulches. This photograph shows part of the main street as the snow begins to melt in spring.

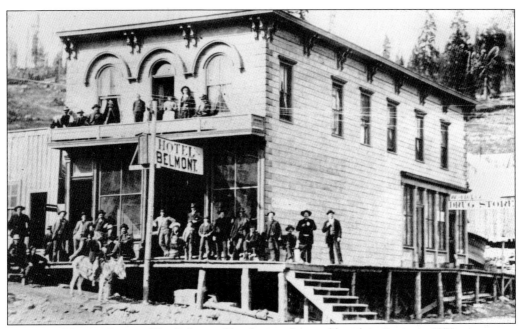

BELMONT HOTEL, IRWIN. The Belmont Hotel, one of several hotels in Irwin in 1882, was a two-story structure with 20 rooms. In the early 1880s, Irwin was the most talked about silver camp in the Gunnison Country. The stage traffic, possibility of a railroad, and activity at the Forest Queen and Bullion King Mines caused great excitement.

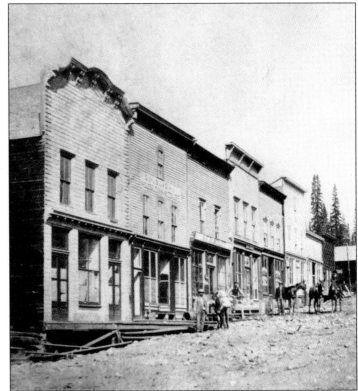

NINTH STREET, IRWIN, 1881. By 1881, Irwin had become a wide-open camp. It was not unusual to find two bands playing at the same time on each end of Main Street. Dance halls were filled to capacity nightly with "Hambone Jane," "Durango Nell," "Cock-eye," and "Timberline Kate" plying their trades.

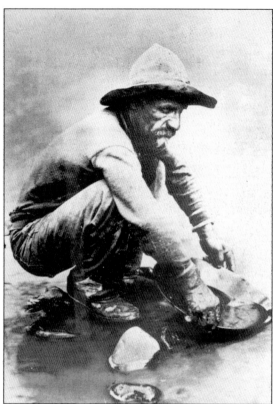

PLACER MINING. Although most of the placer mining in the Gunnison Country occurred from 1860 to 1870, individual prospectors continued to pan main streams. Good returns came from Lottis Creek, Taylor Park, and Washington Gulch. All prospectors were relentless in their quest for pay dirt.

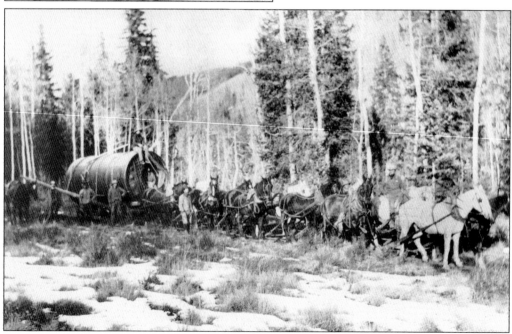

HAULING HEAVY EQUIPMENT INTO TAYLOR PARK. A 12-horse team hauls a heavy boiler over Tin Cup Pass and into Taylor Park in the late spring of 1884. Machinery was often so heavy that it had to be carried to the mines in sections.

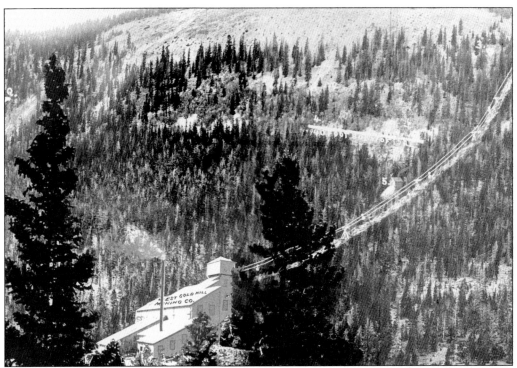

WEST GOLD HILL MINE. The West Gold Hill Mine was located near the 12,015-foot-high Cumberland Pass between the silver towns of Tin Cup and Pitkin. It was a good silver producer with a long tram carrying ore from the mine to the mill.

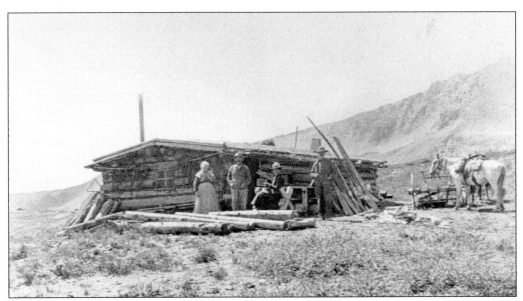

MURDIE'S CABIN. This cabin was built by the Murdie family, which homesteaded land near the head of Spring Creek at the start of the 20th century. The cabin stood near the 10,800-foot-high Reno Divide. Nearby was the good-paying Star Mine and Taylor Park.

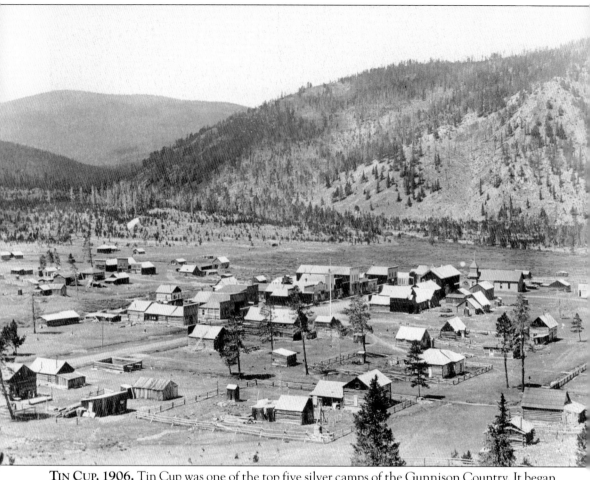

TIN CUP, 1906. Tin Cup was one of the top five silver camps of the Gunnison Country. It began as Virginia City in 1879 but changed its name to Tin Cup in 1882. It was the most lawless of all Gunnison Country camps, as two marshals were gunned down there. At its peak, Tin Cup had a transient population of 4,000.

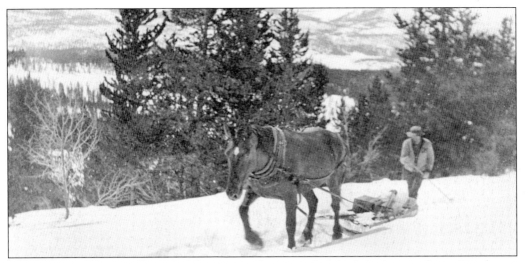

DORCHESTER "FREIGHT," 1908. A lone carrier brings mail and a few other supplies to Dorchester in Taylor Park. Dorchester, located at the north end of the park, was a jumping-off point to Aspen over the 11,800-foot-high Taylor Pass. At its peak in 1910, Dorchester had two stores, two saloons, and a hotel.

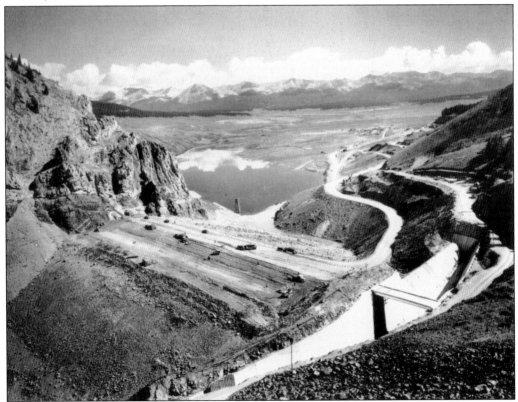

BUILDING TAYLOR DAM. The building of the Taylor Dam from 1935 to 1937 dammed up the Taylor River in the huge park just west of the Continental Divide and created the Taylor Reservoir. The reservoir holds 106,000 acre feet of water that is used for irrigation by farmers of the Uncompahgre Valley near Montrose. The reservoir is also a recreational paradise.

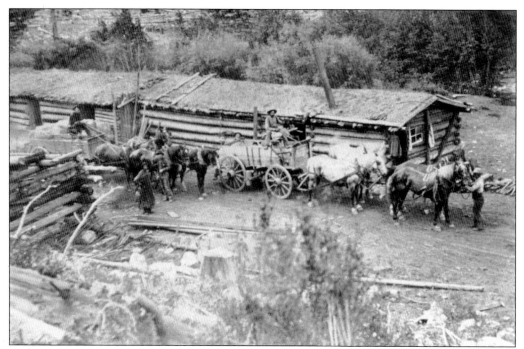

BOGAN'S CAMP. This camp was a halfway point between the famed Doctor Mine, which produced lead and zinc for the World War I effort, and the nearest railroad at Almont. Situated on Spring Creek, it had horse barns and cabins where animals and tired freighters could rest.

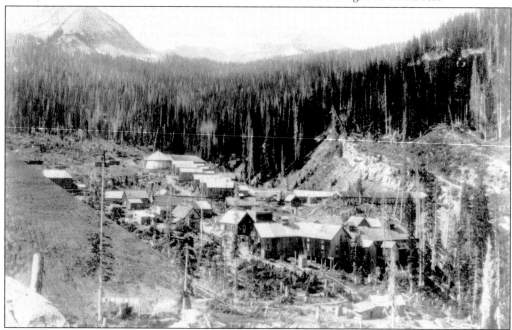

COAL TOWN OF FLORESTA. Originally known as Ruby-Anthracite, Floresta began in 1880 at the head of Anthracite Creek 11 miles west of Crested Butte. It produced anthracite, or hard coal. The arrival of the Denver and Rio Grande Railroad in 1893 ensured Floresta's future. Because of the lessened demand for coal and the harsh weather, however, Floresta died in 1918.

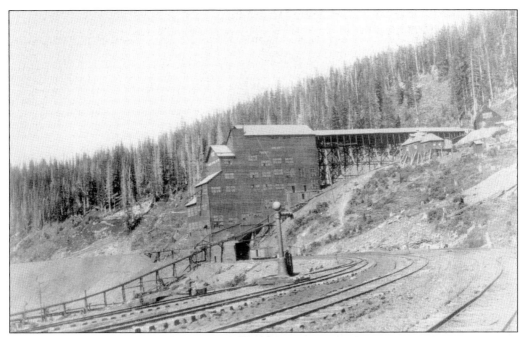

FLORESTA COAL BREAKER. The five-story Floresta coal breaker was constructed in 1898 for $98,000. It was then the largest coal breaker west of Pennsylvania. At 114 feet high, the breaker could handle 2,000 tons of anthracite coal a day. The coal was broken into five different sizes before shipping.

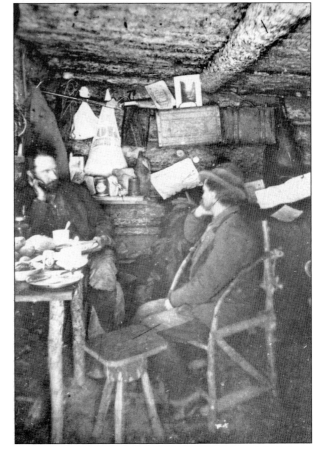

MINER'S CABIN. Shown here is a typical hard rock miner's cabin in the Gunnison Country. This structure stood on Texas Creek in Taylor Park during the 1880s. One can see the bare essentials needed by the miners.

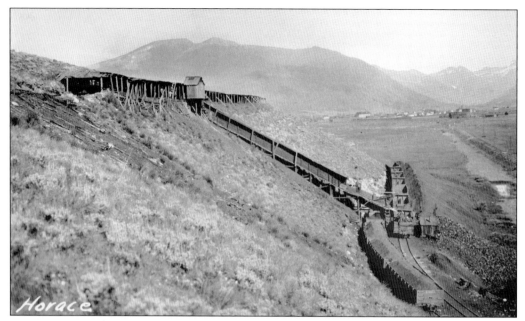

HORACE MINE, CRESTED BUTTE. This mine was located just south of Crested Butte, which is visible in the background. A Denver and Rio Grande train is loading coal below the tipple.

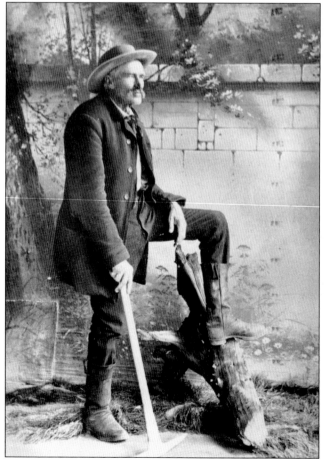

"YANK" BAXTER. "Yank" Baxter was one of the earliest residents of the Gunnison Country, arriving in 1876. A former Argonaut and Pony Express rider, Baxter owned the Excelsior Mine in Poverty Gulch north of Crested Butte. According to locals, his voice was so loud that "it was a divided paying institution before the advent of the telephone."

Eight
CATTLE KINGS AND MINING MEN

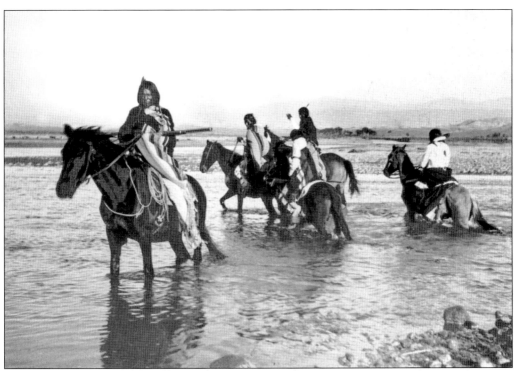

UTE INDIANS. The Ute Indians used the Gunnison Country as a summer range before leaving for the Uncompahgre Valley and warmer climates in winter. During summers in the Gunnison Valley, game was plentiful, rivers were high, and no enemies were near. Here the Utes cross a section of the Gunnison River in the 1870s.

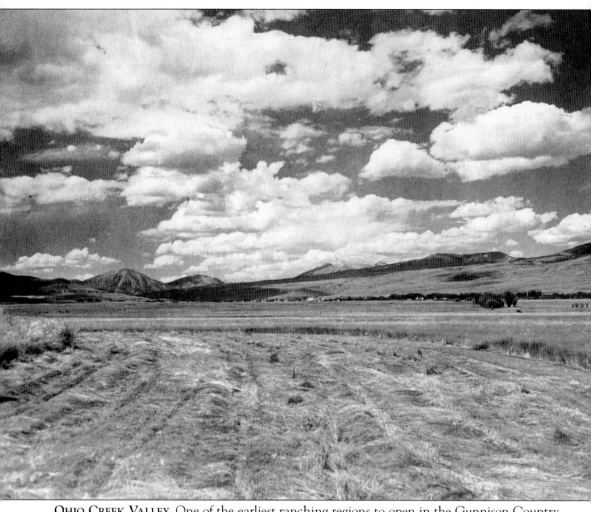

OHIO CREEK VALLEY. One of the earliest ranching regions to open in the Gunnison Country, the Ohio Creek Valley became known for its high-quality hay, its many ranchers, and its coal mines. It was known as the Valley of the Castles because of the nearby mountain rock formation resembling a medieval castle.

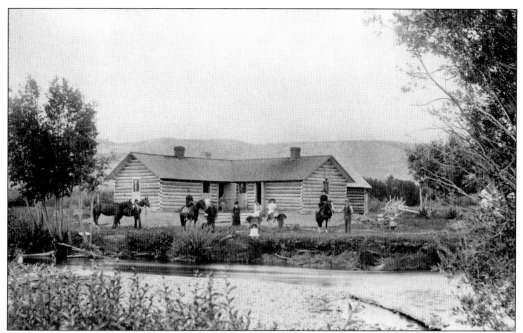

CORNWALL RANCH, OHIO CREEK. Henry and George Cornwall, two brothers from New York, came to the mining camp of Irwin in 1879. They profited from the mines early, but when Irwin declined, they turned to ranching on Ohio Creek. In addition to raising cattle, the Cornwalls also farmed successfully with just a 70-day growing season.

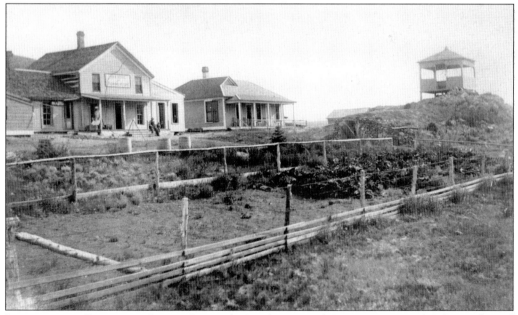

IOLA ON THE GUNNISON RIVER. Located 10 miles west of Gunnison in 1896, Iola was buried by the Blue Mesa Reservoir in the 1960s. Great ranches existed prior to that time, but Iola also became a hunting and fishing mecca with four hotels, a school, a post office, and a general store. When the willow flies hatched on the Gunnison River in the spring, every fisherman in the nation wanted to be in Iola.

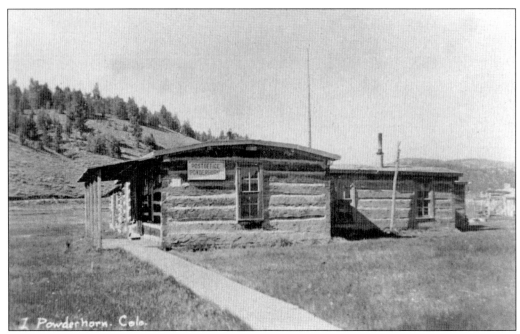

POWDERHORN POST OFFICE. This early log cabin housed the Powderhorn Post Office. The Powderhorn Valley, named for its shape, lies midway between Gunnison and Lake City. Harry Youmans first discovered the potential of the valley in 1873, and it soon became one of the top ranching areas of the Gunnison Country.

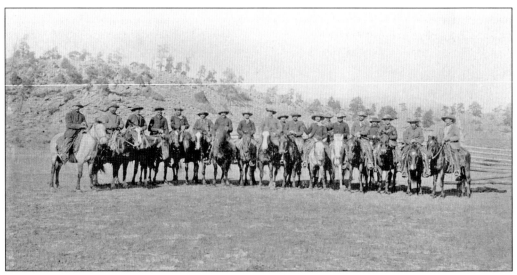

POWDERHORN RANCHERS. This photograph of Powderhorn Valley ranchers was taken in 1884. It depicts most of the historic settlers of the valley, including the Andrews, Stone, Radecka, Sammons, and Bowers families. Cattle outnumbered people in the valley 3,000 to 100. In the fall, Powderhorn ranchers drove their cattle to Iola, where they were loaded onto Denver and Rio Grande trains and taken to market in Denver.

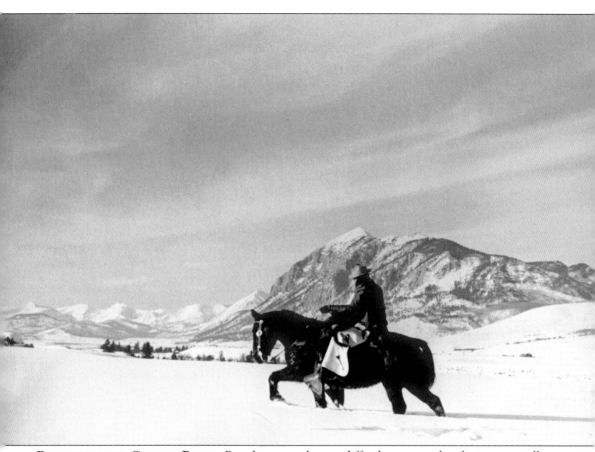

RANCHING NEAR CRESTED BUTTE. Ranching was always a difficult way to make a living, especially during the long and hard winters of the Gunnison Country. In this view, with the Elk Mountains and Mount Crested Butte serving as a backdrop, a rancher rescues a sick calf.

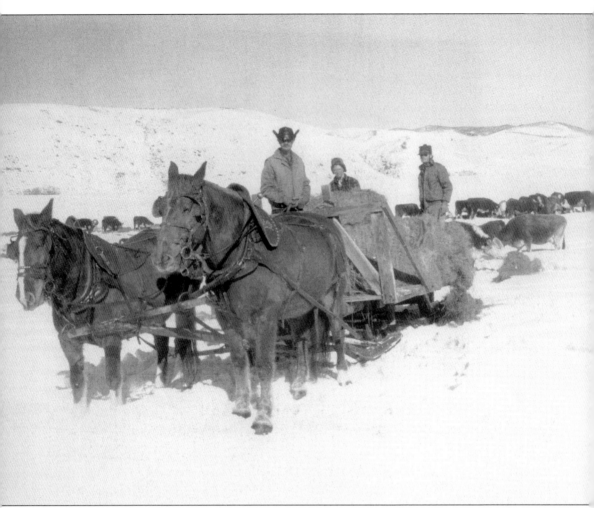

GUNNISON COUNTRY RANCHING. It is feeding time north of Gunnison on a winter morning in the 1950s. Hay is being pushed out of a dray to anxiously waiting cattle. It was not uncommon for temperatures to be consistently 20 degrees below zero on such mornings.

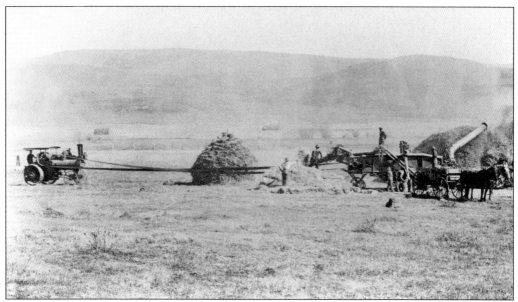

THRESHING ON OHIO CREEK. Fred Eilbrecht's threshing machine and crew are busy in the Ohio Creek Valley in 1913. Though primarily a ranching area, the Gunnison Country also produced many farm commodities in the early years. Wheat, oats, rye, barley, potatoes, lettuce, and strawberries were only some of the crops grown.

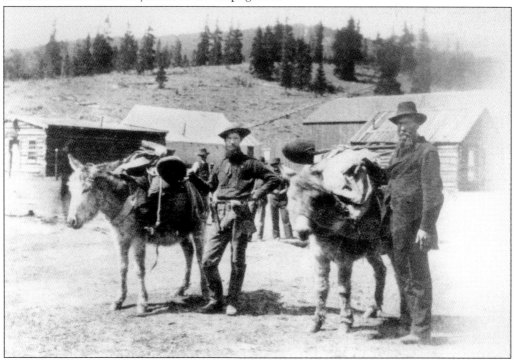

PACKING IN SUPPLIES. Two prospectors with burros loaded prepare to head to their placer diggings in Taylor Park. The little burros, able to pack up to 200 pounds on their backs, were the real heroes of the mining frontier. They were called Rocky Mountain Canaries because when overloaded or in distress, they brayed a shrill whistle that reminded miners of the bird.

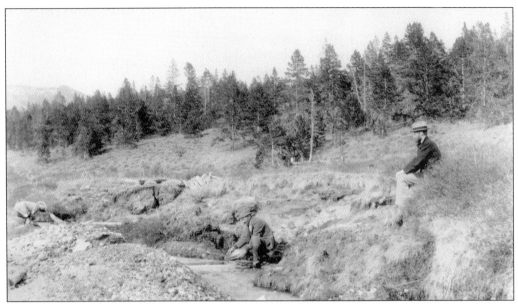

PLACER MINERS. Individual prospectors engage in gold panning on Lottis Creek in the Gunnison Country in the 1880s. The creek was named for placer miner Fred Lottis, who first panned there in 1861.

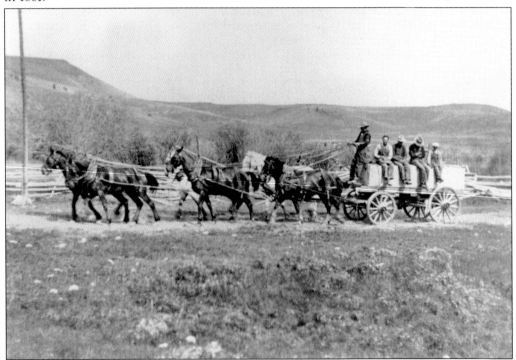

HAULING GRANITE FROM ABERDEEN QUARRY. The Aberdeen granite quarry, six miles southwest of Gunnison, supplied the granite for the construction of the Colorado state capitol. From 1889 to 1892, between 5 and 20 railroad cars of granite were shipped out daily. Before a spur was built from Aberdeen to the Denver and Rio Grande main line, the stone was taken out by wagon. Here Roy Dunbar drives a six-horse team hauling a slab of granite to the railroad.

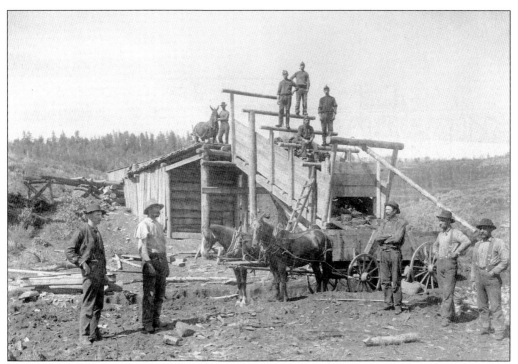

BLACK DIAMOND COAL MINE, OHIO CREEK. A number of small coal mines were worked at the upper end of the Ohio Creek Valley shortly after the Gunnison Country opened in the early 1880s. One of the earliest was the Black Diamond. In this photograph, coal is loaded into a waiting wagon.

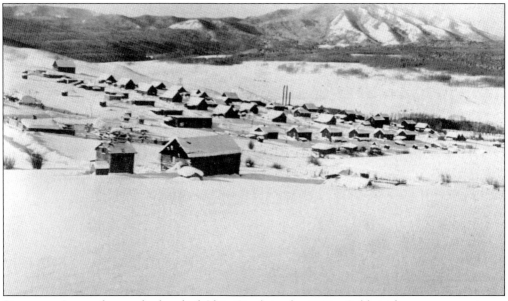

BALDWIN. Located near the head of Ohio Creek in the 1880s, Baldwin became a prominent coal town. The Denver South Park Railroad was accessible, several mines were worked, and the population eventually peaked at 250. Immigrant labor was controlled by the coal companies, leading to many strikes and violence. With the demise of coal, Baldwin shut its doors in 1946.

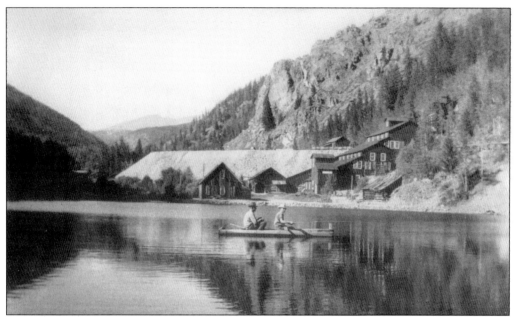

LAKE SAN CRISTOBAL. This beautiful lake just outside Lake City was formed around 1300 when the Slumgullion Slide broke away from a mountainside and dammed up the Lake Fork of the Gunnison River. Lake San Cristobal is the second largest natural body of water in Colorado, surpassed only by Grand Lake. The Golden Fleece Mine is visible in the background.

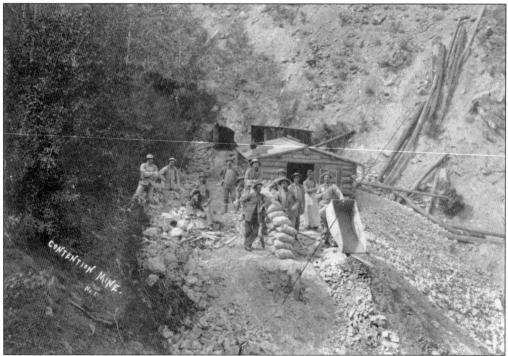

CONTENTION MINE. This gold mine operated near Lake San Cristobal in the 1870s. Local owners sold out to Denver interests in the 1890s and then built a mill to process Contention and other nearby mines' ores. A successful producer, the mine closed early in the 20th century.

Nine
THE BLACK CANYON

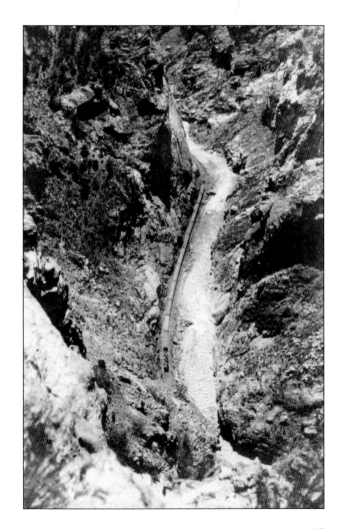

DENVER AND RIO GRANDE TRAIN IN THE BLACK CANYON. Over 2,000 feet below, a barely visible narrow-gauge train picks its way slowly through the Black Canyon with the Gunnison River gnashing its teeth alongside.

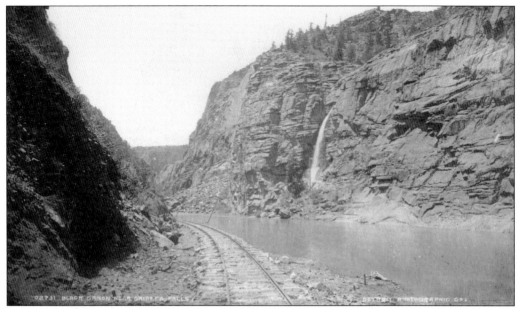

CHIPETA FALLS. Denver and Rio Grande Railroad tracks ran past the beautiful Chipeta Falls, which dropped more than 100 feet from the walls of Black Canyon into the Gunnison River. The falls were located in the canyon between Sapinero and Cimarron, and were named for the wife of Ouray, the Ute Indian chief.

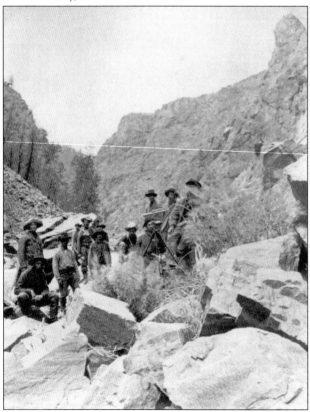

SURVEY TEAM IN BLACK CANYON. William Jackson Palmer of the Denver and Rio Grande Railrod sent a survey team into Black Canyon below Cimarron in 1882. Led by Byron Bryant, the team surveyed the wildest section of the canyon for over two months. Bryant's report declared that it would be impossible to lay tracks there.

CURECANTI NEEDLE. This impressive spire juts upward over 300 feet on the south side of the Gunnison River in Black Canyon. In the 1930s, a small number of Western State College students climbed the Curecanti Needle and placed a flag on top.

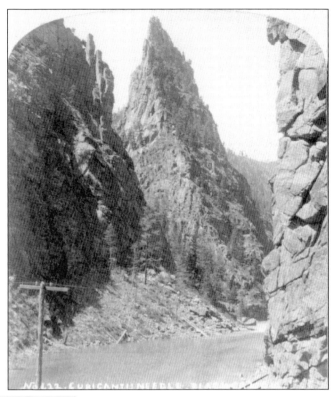

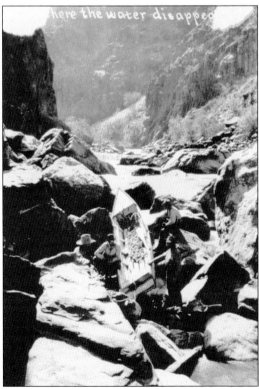

JOHN PELTON'S BLACK CANYON EXPEDITION. In 1900, Montrose rancher John Pelton led a party of five into Black Canyon to see if the Gunnison River could be diverted by a tunnel to the arid Uncompahgre Valley. Pelton took two heavy wooden boats, which had to be portaged most of the time around the roaring waters of the Gunnison River. After 21 days, the explorers gave up 12 miles down the river from Cimarron; they were lucky to escape the canyon.

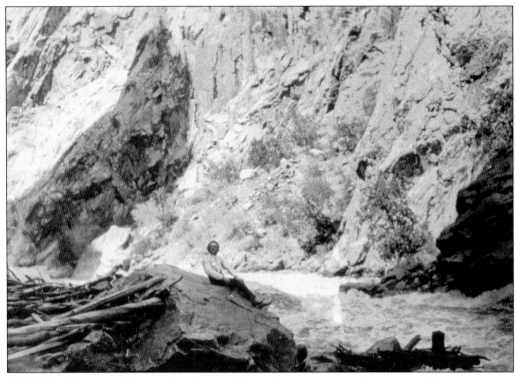

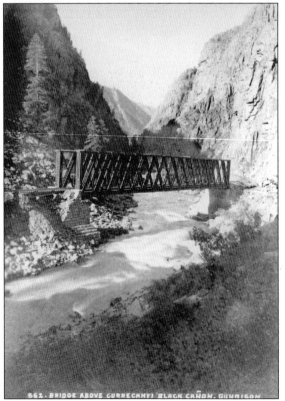

ABRAHAM FELLOWS IN BLACK CANYON. Working for the newly created Reclamation Service, Abraham Lincoln Fellows and William Torrence explored Black Canyon in 1901 and found a tunnel site for the diversion of the Gunnison River. The journey downstream from Cimarron was fraught with danger, and the two men swam across the Gunnison River 76 times. Their expedition led to the building of the 6-mile-long Gunnison Tunnel in 1909. The tunnel diverted the river water and saved the Uncompahgre Valley.

CURECANTI BRIDGE. The Denver and Rio Grande Railroad bridge crossed the Gunnison River just above Curecanti Creek in Black Canyon. This photograph was taken in 1894 when the railroad ran full service through the canyon.

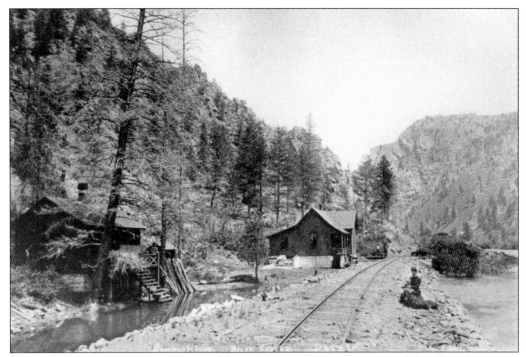

BLACK CANYON, 1886. A woman and her child pose at the Denver and Rio Grande section house in Black Canyon. The section house was located near Curecanti Creek and the Curecanti Needle.

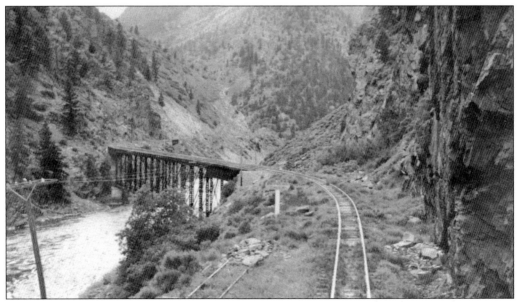

CRYSTAL CREEK, BLACK CANYON. The Denver and Rio Grande tracks crossed from the north to the south side of the Gunnison River near Crystal Creek. At the time of this 1940 view, the great days of the Denver and Rio Grande Railroad were already in the past.

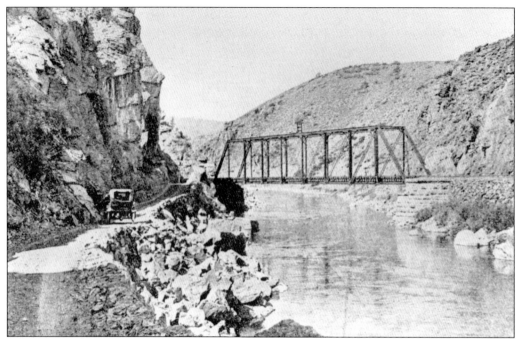

SAPINERO HIGHWAY BRIDGE. The town of Sapinero was at the head of Black Canyon. From Sapinero, the Gunnison River ran 55 miles through the canyon and beyond to its junction with the North Fork at Lazear. This 1915 photograph shows the highway bridge over the Gunnison River near Sapinero. An automobile approaches the bridge.

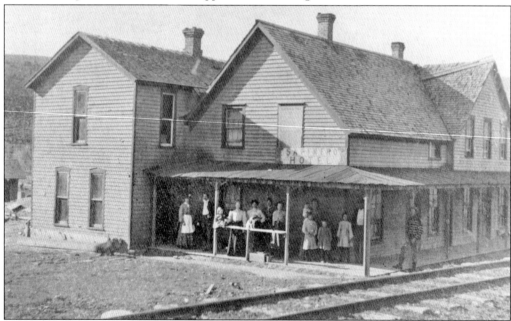

SAPINERO HOTEL. Sapinero was a major stop on the Denver and Rio Grande Railroad. Located 26 miles west of Gunnison, it became an important tourist town because of its access to the Black Canyon. It had two hotels: the Sapinero, pictured here, and the Rainbow. Sapinero was covered with hundreds of feet of water when the Blue Mesa Dam was built in the 1960s.

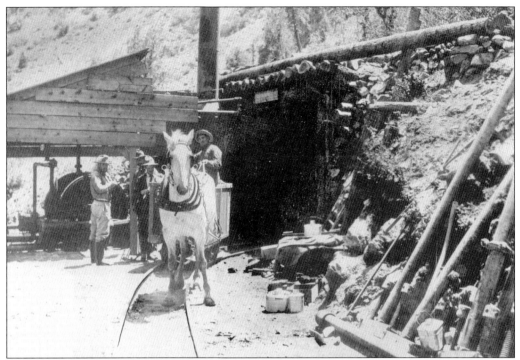

EAST PORTAL, GUNNISON TUNNEL. The Reclamation Service built the 30,583-foot-long Gunnison Tunnel under Vernal Mesa to provide water for the Uncompahgre Valley. In this 1905 view of the east portal, diggings from the tunnel are removed by a primitive horse-drawn mining car.

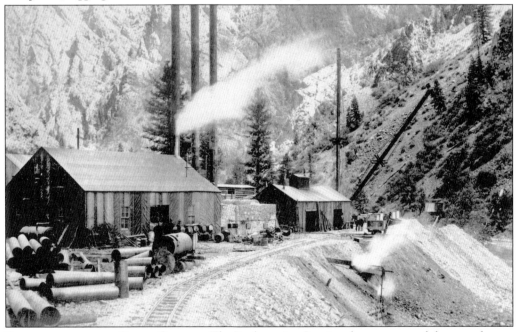

POWERHOUSE IN THE BLACK CANYON. The Reclamation Service also constructed the powerhouse, shown here, at the east portal of the Gunnison Tunnel. It provided power for the workers blasting the tunnel from the Gunnison River westward.

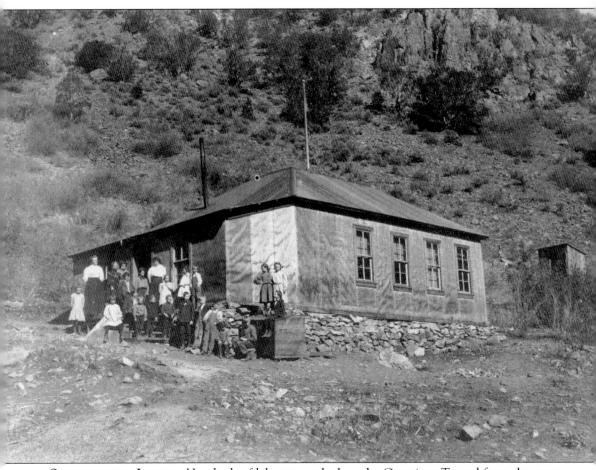

SCHOOLHOUSE, LUJANE. Hundreds of laborers worked on the Gunnison Tunnel from the west portal, also known as Lujane. This primitive building served as a schoolhouse for the children of those workers.

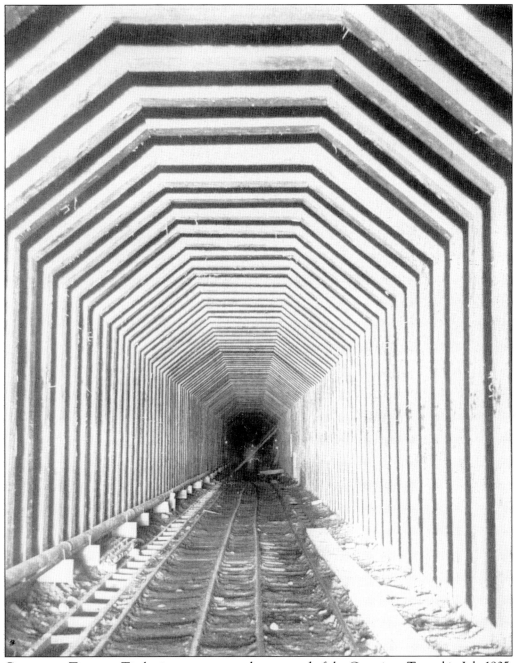
GUNNISON TUNNEL. Timbering occurs near the west end of the Gunnison Tunnel in July 1905. The tunnel work was dangerous due to refractory rock, and 19 men died during construction.

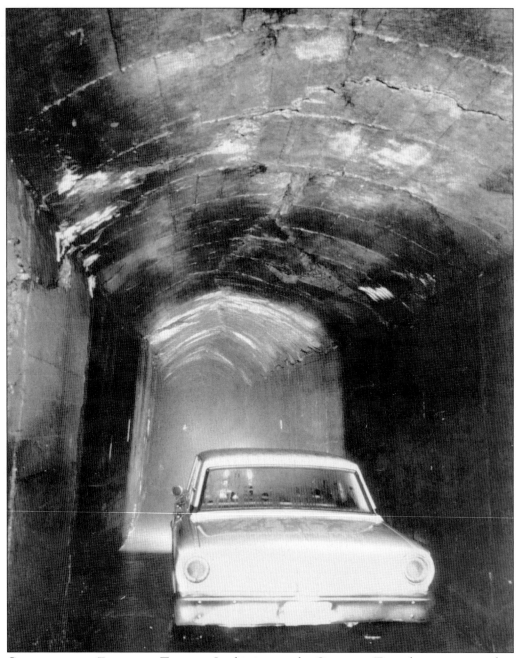

CHECKING THE GUNNISON TUNNEL. In this image, the Gunnison Tunnel is now encased in cement. After Uncompahgre Valley irrigation is finished in the fall, a ditch rider will drive through the six-mile tunnel from the west portal to the east, checking for possible repairs.

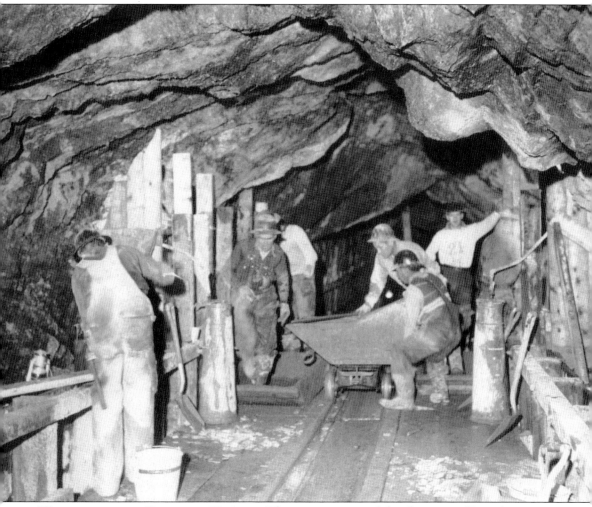

WORKING IN THE GUNNISON TUNNEL. The construction of the Gunnison Tunnel was an engineering marvel. Workers building the tunnel from the west and east portals were only 11 hundredths of an inch off when they met near the middle. These laborers are shown near the center.

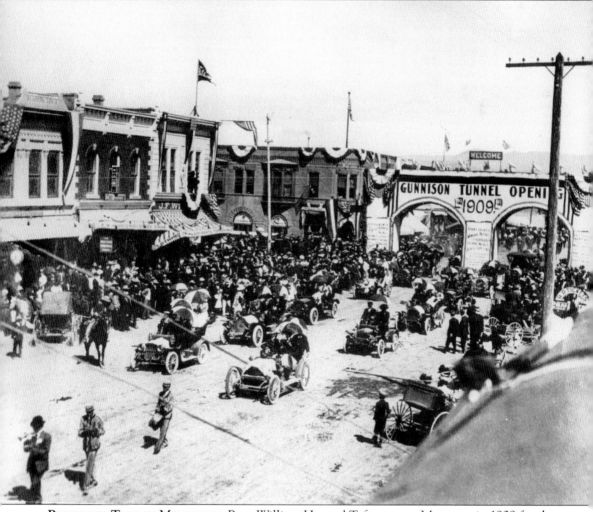

PRESIDENT TAFT IN MONTROSE. Pres. William Howard Taft came to Montrose in 1909 for the dedication of the Gunnison Tunnel. The Uncompahgre Project, as it was known, was the first major reclamation project in the West constructed under the Reclamation Act of 1902. Here President Taft leads a parade down the main street of Montrose.

Ten
Potpourri

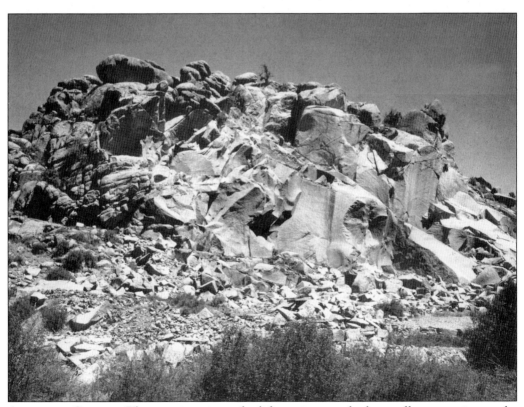

Aberdeen Quarry. This massive piece of solid granite once had a small community nearby during the 1890s. The camp of Aberdeen included a large boardinghouse and a railroad spur running from the quarry to the Denver and Rio Grande Railroad line at Hierro, five miles west of Gunnison.

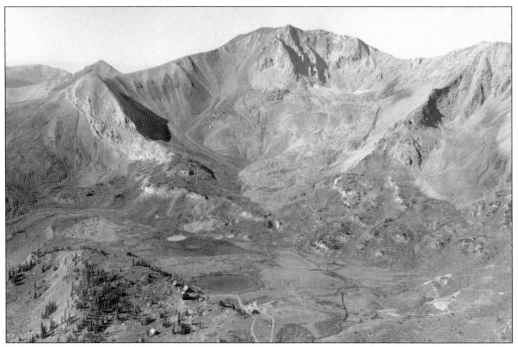

STAR MINE. Surrounded by nearly 14,000-foot-high mountains, the Star Mine opened near the heads of the Springs and Italian Creeks, north and west of Taylor Park, in 1879. A good producer, the Star was owned by Paris socialite Madame Esther LeFebvre from 1911 to 1912.

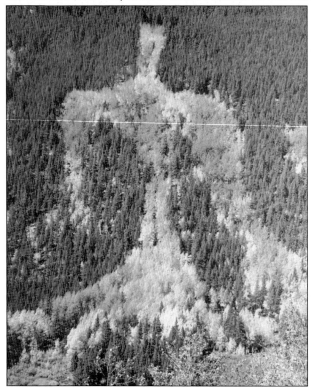

"LIBERTY BELL." Brightly covered aspen trees surrounded by evergreens create a perfect image of a liberty bell near White Pine and Tomichi in the Gunnison Country. Every fall, the view draws camera-toting locals.

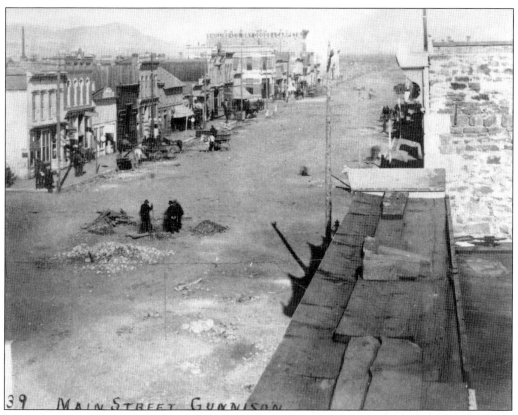

MAIN STREET, GUNNISON. Gunnison was just beginning its boom in the early 1880s when this photograph was taken. Main Street in this view is in rough condition with digging taking place in the center of the street.

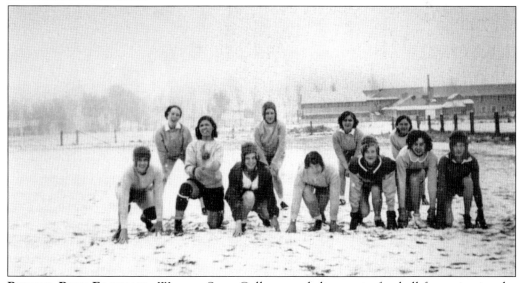

POWDER PUFF FOOTBALL. Western State College coeds line up in football formation on the campus in 1939. The ensuing football game was filmed by Fox Movietone News and shown all over the nation on movie screens.

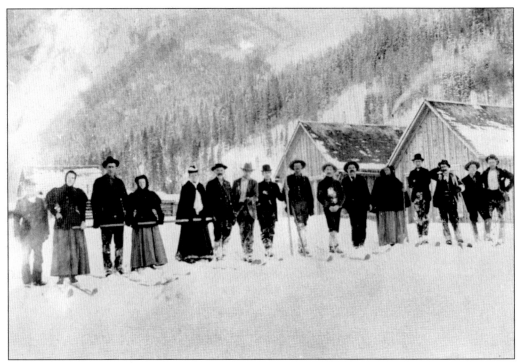

CRYSTAL SNOWSHOE CLUB. Located deep in the Elk Mountains amidst very steep terrain, the Crystal Snowshoe Club became legendary in the Rocky Mountains. It featured many great skiers but none greater than Al Johnson, the famed mail carrier who traveled between Crystal and Crested Butte in the dead of winter through avalanche country.

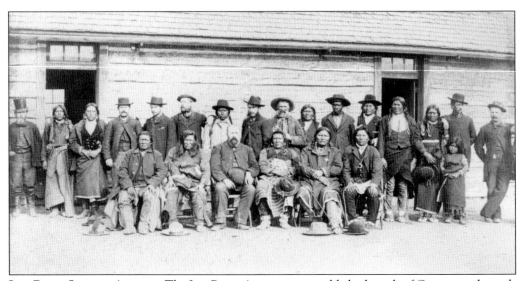

LOS PINOS INDIAN AGENCY. The Los Pinos Agency was established south of Gunnison through the Treaty of 1868. As mining boomed in the Gunnison Country, the Ute Indians were moved to a new reservation at Colona, south of Montrose. They are pictured at Los Pinos with agent Charles Adams (first row, seated third from the left) and other agency employees.

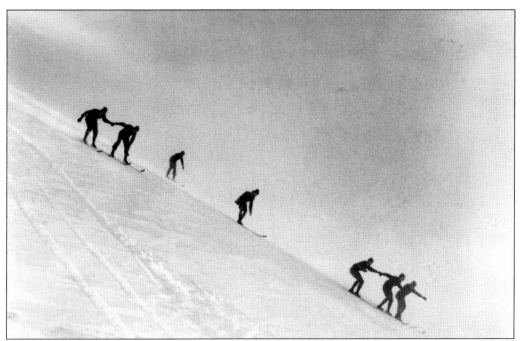

QUICK'S HILL. In this photograph, Western State College students play the dangerous game of "crack the whip" on Quick's Hill near the Glacier School in 1932. The skiers are all members of the Hiking and Outing Club.

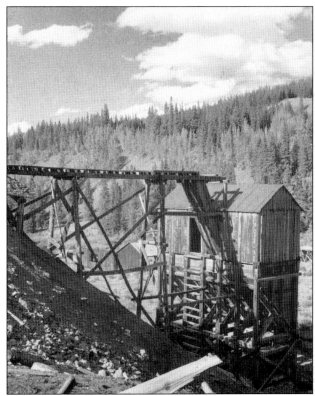

GOLD CUP MINE. Remains of the historic Gold Cup Mine are seen here. The mine opened on Gold Hill near Tin Cup in 1879 and became one of the top 10 silver producers in Gunnison Country history.

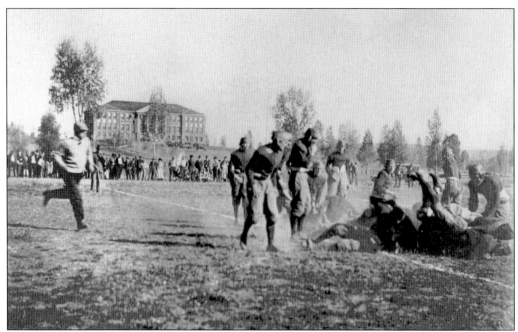

FOOTBALL GAME, 1919. With Taylor Hall in the background, the Colorado State Normal School football team plays Canyon City to a 0-0 tie in Gunnison on October 26, 1919. Four years later, the college became a four-year institution and was renamed Western State College.

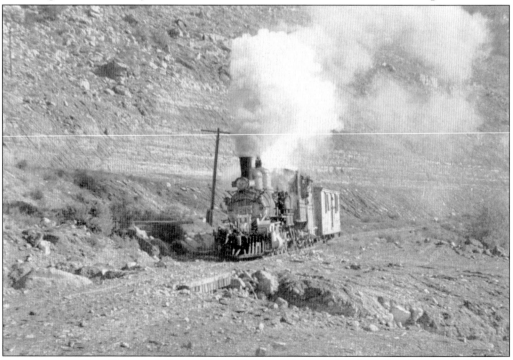

DENVER AND RIO GRANDE'S LAST RUN. The era of the railroad in the Gunnison Country would be over shortly after this ride. The engine makes its last run near Cebolla Creek, west of Gunnison, in 1954.

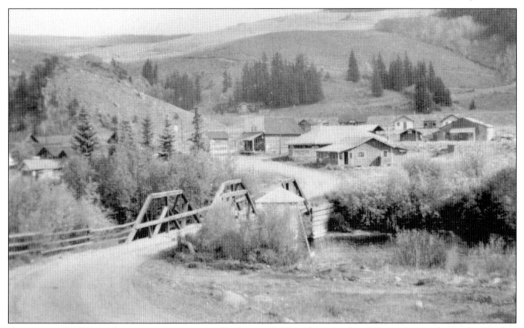

ALMONT, 1940s. Almont was strategically located 10 miles north of Gunnison where the Taylor and East Rivers joined to form the headwaters of the Gunnison River. Started by Sam Fisher in 1879, it became a halfway station for freighters and miners going to the Elk Mountains and promising silver mines. Today it is a resort village.

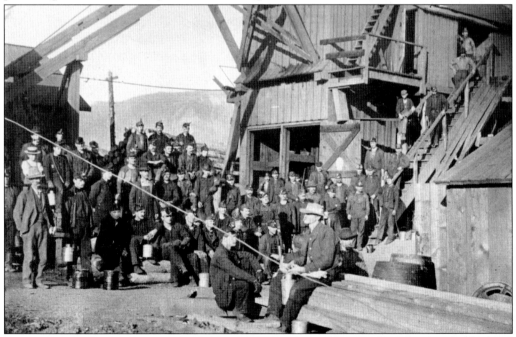

KUBLER MINE TIPPLE, 1898. The Kubler Coal Mine opened on Carbon Creek near the head of the Ohio Creek Valley in 1881. This photograph shows coal miners at Kubler. Over 100 men were employed at the Rocky Mountain Fuel Company mine, which was served by the Denver South Park Railroad.

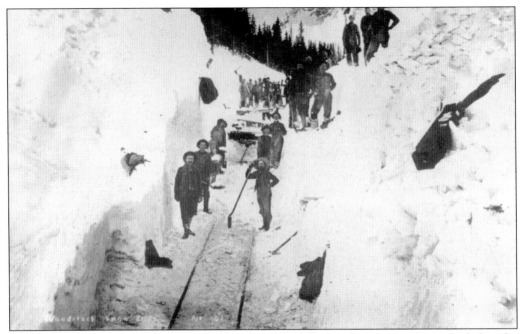

WOODSTOCK SLIDE. Woodstock was a Denver South Park Railroad settlement four miles below the Alpine Tunnel. On March 10, 1884, an avalanche completely wiped out the little camp and killed 14 people, including 6 from one family. Here workers clear the railroad tracks after the disaster.

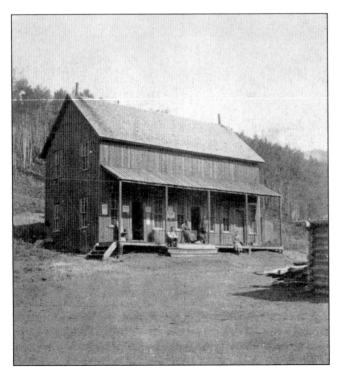

KING'S RANCH, JUNE, 28, 1881. King's Ranch was a halfway point between Gunnison and the silver camp of Irwin to the north. The ranch included a dance hall, a huge corral, and two barns. Weary freighters and travelers stopped there for the night before continuing their ascent of the 10,033-foot-high Ohio Pass the next morning.

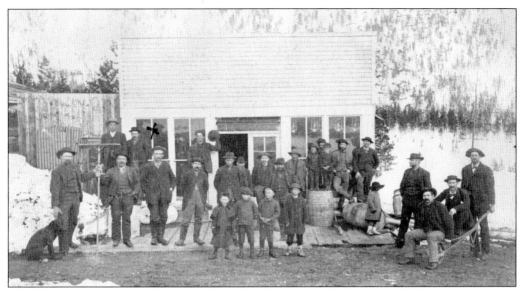

TURNER AND MACY STORE, 1884. This general store was one of the few frame buildings in the White Pine silver camp in the early 1880s. Because of the town's good-paying mines, the population grew to more than 1,000 by 1884. A decade later, the silver panic caused the town to be deserted.

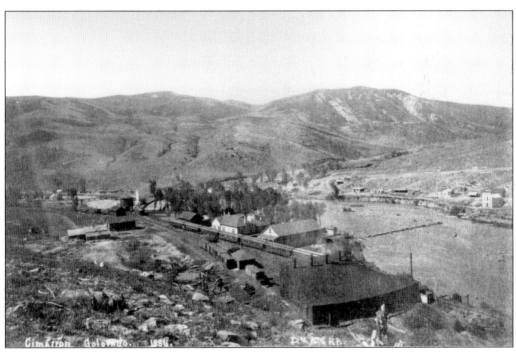

CIMARRON, 1886. Cimarron was where the Denver and Rio Grande Railroad was forced to leave the rugged Black Canyon. From there, the railroad ran over Cierro Summit to Montrose in 1882. At its peak in the early 1880s, Cimarron had a general store, three restaurants, a dance hall, and 11 saloons.

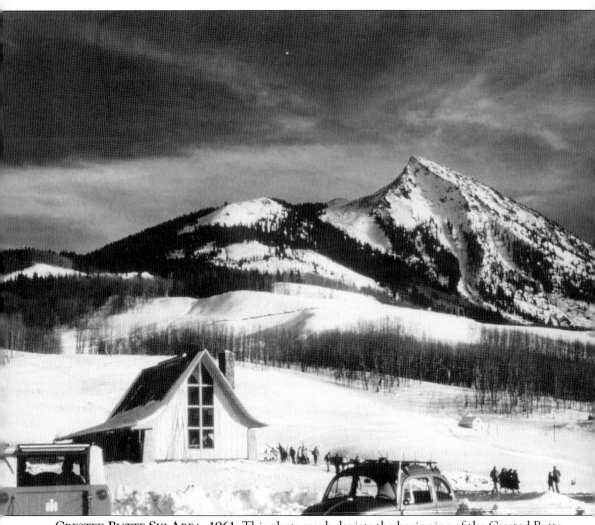

CRESTED BUTTE SKI AREA, 1961. This photograph depicts the beginning of the Crested Butte Ski Area. The new area opened on a shoestring during the winter of 1961–1962, the dream of Dick Eflin and Fred Rice. The nearly completed warming house is in the foreground, and the J-Bar building appears in the background.

BIBLIOGRAPHY

Borneman, Walter R. *Irwin: Silver Camp of the Ruby Mountains*. Western State College, Gunnison, CO: unpublished master's thesis, 1975.

Carnahan, John. *History of Ohio City, Colorado, 1860–1920*. Western State College, Gunnison, CO: unpublished typescript, 1969.

Class of 1916. *Historical Sketches of Early Gunnison*. Gunnison, CO: Colorado State Normal School, 1916.

Frost, Frank P., ed. *Scenes in and about Marble, Colorado*. Marble, CO: Marble Booster, 1883.

Hallowell, John K. *Gunnison: Colorado's Bonanza Country*. Denver: Colorado Museum of Applied Geology and Mineralogy, 1883.

Hartman, Alonzo. *Remembrances of Pioneer Days in the Gunnison Country*. Unpublished typescript, 1900.

Jack, Ellen E. *The Fate of a Fairy*. Chicago: M. A. Donohue and Company, 1910.

Jocknick, Sidney. *Early Days on the Western Slope of Colorado*. Denver: Carson-Harper Company, 1913.

Lathrop, Gilbert. *Little Engines and Big Men*. Caldwell, ID: Caxton Printers, 1954.

McCanne, David J. *Memoirs of a Civil Engineer*. Denver: unpublished typescript, 1937.

Nelson, A. P. *Gunnison County, Colorado*. Pitkin, CO: A. P. Nelson Mining, 1916.

Root, George A. "A Boy in Colorado: Memoirs of Gunnison, 1881–1885." *American History Illustrated* VI, No. 7 (November 1971): 23–30.

Vandenbusche, Duane, and Rex Myers. *Marble, Colorado: City of Stone*. Denver: Golden Bell Press, 1970.

Wallace, Betty. *The Gunnison Country*. Denver: Sage Books, 1960.

———. *History with the Hide Off*. Denver: Sage Books, 1964.

Across America, People are Discovering Something Wonderful. *Their Heritage.*

Arcadia Publishing is the leading local history publisher in the United States. With more than 4,000 titles in print and hundreds of new titles released every year, Arcadia has extensive specialized experience chronicling the history of communities and celebrating America's hidden stories, bringing to life the people, places, and events from the past. To discover the history of other communities across the nation, please visit:

www.arcadiapublishing.com

Customized search tools allow you to find regional history books about the town where you grew up, the cities where your friends and family live, the town where your parents met, or even that retirement spot you've been dreaming about.

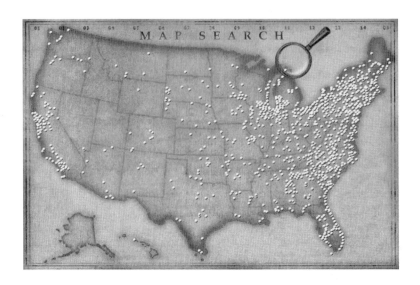